THE ACCIDENTAL CEO

THE ACCIDENTAL CEO

A Leader's Journey from Ego to Purpose

TOM VOCCOLA

Sea Fever Press
Thousand Oaks, Ca.

For information, address
tvoccola@ceo2.com
Sea Fever Press books may be purchased for educational,
business, or sales promotion use.
For information, please contact tvoccola@ceo2.com

FIRST EDITION

Library of Congress Cataloging-in-Publication data

Voccola, Thomas Anthony 1945 –
The Accidental CEO: A Leader's Journey from Ego to Purpose/ Tom Voccola. – 1st ed.
Paperback includes appendix and index.
ISBN: 978-1-4116-8857-5
1. Leadership 2. Organizational Change 3. Business. 4. Self Help

This book is dedicated to the
Art of Personal & Corporate Transformation

"Every man must be his own leader.
He now knows enough not to follow other people.
He must follow the light that's within himself,
and through this light
he will create a new community.

— Laurens Van Der Post

ACKNOWLEDGEMENTS

Through all its permutations, *The Accidental CEO* has taken me more than five years to write. I thank God for His timely revelation that I had to *be the book* before I could write it.

I thank Melissa Cook for her remarkable ability to take a raw manuscript and not only make it intelligible, but add heart, depth and understanding to it.

I thank Doug Brown for his superb editing and his much appreciated suggestions and encouragement.

Thank you Dr. Douglas Markham, Paul Deis and G.E. Nordell for helping take the mystery out of writing, and Kapaka Senko, my Oracle, for telling me exactly what I needed to hear when I needed to hear it.

To the hundreds of CEOs and leaders I've worked with, interviewed and learned from over the years, especially Dick Hardy, Ralph Lawrence, Don Cummings, David Wilson, Harry Neiman, Jim McGovern, David Berg, Dr. Jack O'Malley, Steve Kaplan, Barbara Fitzgerald, Frank Ferratta, Ted Myers, Ray Inge, Al Erkert, E. Michael Thoben III, Rami Musallum, Rev. Sue Rubin, the late George Van Ness, Doug Dickey, Thomas Wendt and Curtis Overstreet, for being open to a new possibility and having the courage to be authentic. And thank you, Merritt Lutz, for giving me so much to work with.

Thanks to my AeA CEO Group: E. Michael Thoben III, Jason Carlson, Peter Cassady, Derek Cheung, Ron Means, Tony Radaich, Martin Shum, Fred Strum, Gerald Shane and Jim Westchester. You guys are priceless.

A special thanks to Osamu (Sammy) Tsukada for bringing CEOing and his passion for Global Dignity to Japan.

Thanks to my good friend Bill Wagner at *Accord Management Systems* for continuing to teach me about personalities and myself.

Thank you Jeff Rigsby and Guy Greco for the amazing tools of *Virtual CEO.*

I am so grateful to all the managers and employees of every company and organization that has taken these ideas and made them come alive at every level in the workplace over the past 15 years. Thank you for your daily inspiration and passion.

I acknowledge Werner Erhard as the catalyst for my own transformation, and Denis Waitley, David Gordon, Robert Dilts, Robert Allen, Mark Victor Hansen, Jay Conrad Levinson, Dan Sullivan, T. Harv Eker and Neale Donald Walsh for bringing so much to the world by pioneering new and exciting ways to bring self-awareness to people. You have been my mentors and I thank you from the bottom of my heart.

A profound thank you to John McNeil for teaching me that energy always follows focus, and for introducing me to the wonderful world of management and leadership consulting.

Deepest gratitude to those who took the time to read the first drafts and helped me expand and refine dialog, especially my wife Frances Fujii, my sailing partners Brett Modesti and Norm Jansen whose loving and generous hearts have made such a tremendous impact on me, and Linda Leviton, Steve Gomes, Preston Buck, Doug Workings, Mark Strauch, Dennis Gomes, Pam Popielarski, Chuck Coonradt, Ron Werft and Jay Levinson for your generous support and encouragement.

My deepest gratitude goes to my wife, soulmate, business partner, co-creator and final editor Frances Fujii – without your support, encouragement and inspiration I would have never found my own voice and this book would still be an idea sitting in the back of my mind.

I thank my friend and business partner George Senko for being there through it all, and the rest of the CEO^2 team, Beverly Mineo, Steve Gomes, Fred Jorge, Ed & Sharlene Wein, Rosemary Wellonen and Ilaria Vilkelis for your commitment to our work, even when things looked bleak.

And, last but never least; I thank my parents, Edwin and Catherine Voccola, my children, Jennifer, Jean Marie, Christopher and Mei-Ling, and my amazing grandson Chai, for your love, support and inspiration.

INTRODUCTION

WHAT IF YOU KNEW?

"For everything we know, and for everything we know that we don't know,
there is an entire universe of information that we don't even know that we don't know.
It's in this realm that transformation occurs."
– Werner Erhard

What if you suddenly learned that you were born to do something magnificent – something that could change the world for the better in your lifetime? Would you do it?

Many of us secretly wish that we could be the hero up on the big screen, but we also figure *it's never going to happen.* But what if it could? Would you step into that role? Or would you pull back, deciding it was too hard? Would you think, "I have too much invested in my life the way it is to risk changing things," or "Who am I to do this?" or "Who would ever believe in *me*?"

I'm going to share something with you that few in business – or in the world for that matter – will ever tell you. You *are* here to change the world in your lifetime, and it's time you found out exactly how, because while you may not be consciously aware of it, you already have all of the inner resources you need to make it happen.

This book is about Leadership and Creating Extraordinary Organizations. It's also about how each of us can attain self fulfillment, rewarding relationships – and change the world in our lifetimes.

The inspiration for this book came from the thousands of men and women in the workplace that my partners, Frances Fujii, George Senko and I have worked with over the past fifteen years. Time and again, we've seen people reach deep *inside* to create miracles, powerful relationships and compelling Visions of the future.

While *The Accidental CEO* is fiction, it is based on a compilation of true stories and events that illustrate how one man finds his true calling and then helps an entire organization do the same. As the story unfolds, you will be introduced to tools and a new perspective on leading organizations that will make it possible for you to duplicate his success – for yourself and your organization. But believe it or not, finding out why you are here and learning how to transform large organizations are the easy parts. The real test of leadership lies with the question: When you find out what you are here to do, will you have the courage to embrace it?

If you are holding this book in your hands, I believe you can. Let me know how it goes.

Tom Voccola
Aboard Sea Fever
March 15, 2006

tvoccola@ceo2.com
www.ceo2.com

THE ACCIDENTAL CEO

CHAPTER 1

SUNRISE

Slow motion time warps signal a dawning of awareness.

Sunrise revealed a blood-red sky stained with pitch-black smoke from the oil fires. They had been traveling all night without a break. In spite of the heat, smoke and uncertainty, he and his troops were alert. He had every intention of surviving this thing. But nothing prepared him for the Rocket Propelled Grenade that slammed into the door of his Humvee. The sudden impact scared the hell out of him. He looked down and saw the smoking round sticking through the door five inches from his hip. Miraculously, it didn't detonate.

All hell broke loose with the dull thud of bullets hitting metal, and fountains of sand flying into the air as small arms and machine gun fire bracketed his vehicle. He jumped out the drivers side with his radio man, Jeff Harper, in tow, and began deploying his men and getting a handle on the situation. As he did, Lieutenant Bob Harris entered a slow motion time warp where everything became clear, and there was no fear. Standing upright, he moved with the calm confidence of a seasoned warrior, machine gun fire crashing all around him. He pointed and his men responded. He spoke and it happened. It was over in less than five minutes.

The enemy didn't have a chance.

CHAPTER 2

EVOLUTION

"Personal mastery means approaching one's life as a creative work,
living life from a creative as opposed to reactive viewpoint."
- Peter Senge

Robert W. Harris was born into a reactive world, an eye-for-an-eye world filled with fear, uncertainty and doubt. Of course, he wasn't aware of this. It was just the way things were. He was born with a strong Ego to protect him, as well as a strong Purpose with which to guide his life here on earth. Like all humans, he came as a contribution to his species. He was born a teacher with a unique message to express in the world. But he wasn't aware of this either. Nor would he be for a long time to come.

As might be expected, his parents were already trained in the ways of the world. His father and mother began to teach him how to protect himself from his surroundings and what not to do in this world to get along. "Don't do this" and "don't do that." He learned not to trust strangers; how to always be wary and on his guard.

Robert's teachers, mentors and society in general, continued his instruction in self-defense and reinforced his Ego time and time again. He was also instructed about who to be as well. "Be a good boy, be a gentleman," his mother guided. "Be a hard worker, be strong and take it like a man," his father said. "Be like George Washington and never tell a lie," his teacher admonished. "Be vigilant and watch your back," his sergeant major warned. "Take on the seven habits of highly successful people," said his boss.

Yet no one ever addressed that part of him called Purpose, and so it lay dormant, while his Ego became stronger, more dominant and powerful. He learned how to be effective in reactive environments. He developed his Ego mask and became a hero called Bob Harris.

He was encouraged to win at every turn. He worked to be

faster, stronger, and smarter. He loved sports and attended UCLA on a football scholarship, where he excelled as a quarterback and even took the team to the championships in both his junior and senior years. Good grades came easy, and he graduated at the top of his class as a business major.

He made it out of UCLA's Anderson School of Management, completing his MBA just in time to participate in the first Gulf War as a Marine second lieutenant, bouncing around the Iraqi desert for 8 months as a Heavy Weapons platoon commander. He survived that ordeal as well, although not without a few scars to his psyche. Seemingly unstoppable, he tackled his life with confidence. Resourceful, capable, and in control, he was seen by his peers and superiors at work as a leader, although he was, in reality, a *master of reaction* able to handle whatever his reactive world could throw at him. He became adept at saving the project, saving the sale, saving the client and saving the day. He found himself always out in front fighting to win, to survive.

Every once in a while, however, he had a nagging sense that there was something more, some reason for his success; but he never stopped to question it, because there was always the next hill to take. He unconsciously wielded his Ego as a sword, because in his world view, everything looked like an enemy to be conquered. He was very, very good at attacking whatever came his way, whatever was next.

Until he became a CEO.

CHAPTER 3

THE ACCIDENTAL CEO

"There is no training to be a CEO; it's an extraordinary thing."
— Gerald Levin, former CEO, AOL Time Warner, Inc.

B usiness is among the most reactionary environments in the world. It's been said that those of strong will and quick reflexes are the winners on the court and in the Board room. Bob certainly seemed to have it all. He was a practiced winner, and why not? His company gave him all the practice he needed to "save the day" over and over again. After the Marines, Bob went to work at Arthur Andersen as an analyst in their supply chain practice. Within two years he found himself on the fast track at Andersen, but decided to switch to Deloitte to become a Strategy Practice Team Leader. That's where he met Jim Wellington, a hot shot college professor at Boston University. Jim was on Deloitte's Academic Resource staff. Over lunch one day, Jim told Bob that he and a few investors were pursuing a software approach for identifying and managing mission critical corporate projects. The system would dramatically improve enterprise visibility within increasingly distributed organizations. The rest was history. When Jim made the jump from academia to start Corporate Insights (CI) he and Bob kept in touch. Two years later, when the new company began to experience success, Bob got the call and he took over Sales. Although this was a new position for him, he was a natural and was helped immensely by his consulting experience. Within two years, CI was ready to go public.

After another two years, CI was a leading player in the growing project management space, and Bob Harris became the company's top fire fighter. After assisting with the acquisition of a key competitor, PDQ, Bob was asked to move from VP Domestic Sales to VP/GM of European Operations, to help the company recoup lost revenue after they lost their largest European client to the competition.

Only one year into his new assignment, on an overcast Thursday in January, Bob was notified of yet another corporate fire: founder and CEO Jim Wellington announced he was leaving.

Bob was requested to attend an emergency Board meeting the day after the announcement. He had his assistant cancel all his appointments for the next few days and caught the red eye from London to New York and then on to Chicago. As he sat in the 8 A.M. meeting, his fatigued mind drifted back over the tumultuous events of the past 12 months.

One year earlier, when Jim asked Bob to transfer, he wasn't happy with becoming involved with the struggling European operation. It was, as far as Bob could see, primarily a sales issue, which the previous European sales guy had been unable to manage effectively. Jim convinced Bob it was critical to CI's survival in Europe and added that the General Management title and experience would be good for Bob's career. When Bob transferred to the European position, the Sales VP from the recent PDQ acquisition, Bill Peters, replaced him. As Bob had anticipated, the European mission was primarily focused on PR, sales and service since marketing, software development and global support were still handled out of the U.S.

But the job was far from being a cake walk. After a year Bob was turning things around but was also running himself and his people ragged. None of them would be able to keep up the pace much longer. Unfortunately, his requests for more support and people had been put on hold three times while the parent organization went through its own growing pains. So far, however, he'd acted as a buffer: his people were still on the optimistic side, and Jim and the Board were pleased with his progress. The good news was his group was only supposed to focus on sales and customer service. The bad news was that the domestic group was dropping the ball in product development and global technical support. Bob's group was having serious problems getting their customer requirements into the new software development queue, which seriously jeopardized expanding existing customer sales. This left the European division feeling like a stepchild. The PDQ acquisition wasn't living up to expectations.

Jim had lobbied to buy PDQ to acquire their obvious software talent and cut the development time to CI's next software release. PDQ's legendary breakthroughs in new applications allowed real-time enterprise visibility and were supposed to save three years of development.

Integrating PDQ into CI hadn't come without a lot of pain. Bill Rittman, one of the original bright lights behind CI's initial success, who'd worked his way up from Applications Engineer to Development VP, was replaced by favored Chris Cooper, Development VP from PDQ. Bill was a great applications engineer, but when promoted to VP at CI, he'd stumbled badly. When he was asked to leave the company, a good number of his original staff were let go with him, which created serious morale issues. Bob had liked Bill, but realized that these things happen in mergers and acquisitions. It was too bad, but there was nothing he could do about it. Furthermore, the PDQ people, who were pretty much concentrated in the Development department in Portland, Oregon, for some as yet unknown reason, were acting really defensive. Simple requests from the rest of the company were being turned into battles at every level.

"*Bob…*"

Suddenly, Bob was jolted out of his reverie as he heard his name spoken.

"*…we want you to take over as interim CEO while we conduct a search for a new CEO. In the meantime you need to stop the bleeding and get us on solid footing with the PDQ acquisition.*"

Phil Devine, a founding partner with Devine, Knight & Morris, (DKM) venture capitalists out of Los Angeles and one of Corporate Insights' largest shareholders, delivered the news.

"I know this request is from left field Bob, but the Board has a lot of confidence in your ability to handle it, especially after your experience in Europe. Let's get together after the meeting and I'll fill you in on what we want you to do."

"Sure, I think, I mean, I don't understand, how come…what happened to Jim?" Bob stammered to an uncharacteristically sloppy close.

Phil just smiled at him, "I understand this is sudden, but I think its best we talk off-line, Bob. Let's get together after the meeting."

The rest of the meeting focused on handling the press and making the transition as painless as possible. The official version would be that Jim would be leaving to spend more time with his family. Bob would find out later that there was more truth to the official statement than he thought.

On the way out of the Board meeting Bob looked into Jim's empty office. Bob had had a great deal of respect for his boss. Jim had grown Corporate Insights from his living room coffee table into an $80 million firm in just six years. Three years ago, Bob had worked closely with Jim to help with the IPO. He knew Jim had been having serious problems integrating the PDQ acquisition but never thought Jim would decide to leave the company. Sure, everyone was stretched to the max, but what was unusual about that? It was just part of the business, especially in this market. Besides, Jim always seemed to pull things off. "How does the founder end up leaving his own company?" he thought. "What could have been that bad?"

Bob thought for a brief moment of going in and sitting down at Jim's desk but he didn't feel comfortable with that. Not yet. "Hell the body isn't even cold," he thought.

Just then Rebecca Murray, Jim's executive assistant, came up behind him, took him by the arm and walked him the final few steps into Jim's office and closed the door. She had been in the meeting and knew what had happened. Rebecca had been with Jim from the beginning and was a real firecracker. Part of the problem, she knew, was that the acquisition was going badly, although few yet knew how badly.

"Can we talk, Bob?"

"Sure Rebecca," said Bob.

"Well, since Jim decided to leave, I was just wondering if I still have a job. Do you want me to resign?"

"No, don't be silly. Besides, you can help me get up to speed faster than anyone I can think of." said Bob. "Why don't we both spend the weekend getting used to this new situation and meet on Monday first thing to handle any fires? I'll need to know everything Jim was working on that I may not be aware of before I go home tonight. Can you handle that?"

"I have it right here," she answered, handing Bob six labeled folders. Each folder had a project statement on the left side and the appropriate correspondence and material laid out on the right in chronological order. "I think you should speak with Neil about the financials right away. I spoke with him earlier, and he's ready for you if you can connect later today."

Neil Coulter was CI's CFO. Bob was thankful for Rebecca's organizational skills.

"Thanks, Rebecca. And, by the way, we'd better get all of Jim's direct reports in here right after you and I meet on Monday. I know it's early, but I'd like to meet with you from 7 to 8 and then have the staff meeting begin at 8:15 A.M. Will you schedule things?"

"No problem," said Rebecca, "not everyone knows yet. Those who do are in shock, so they're going to be anxious to get together to see what's happening. I'll put it on their handhelds. They'll know within the hour. Shall I plan on attending the staff meeting as well?"

"You go where I go, Rebecca."

Bob went back to his temporary 'virtual' office. The way the company was set up he could be on line with company servers in moments and access any project, file or person from anywhere in the world. "We're supposed to be leaders in corporate insight, but we sure didn't see this coming," thought Bob. "I guess we still have a way to go on creating reliable corporate visibility in our own company. What we really need is corporate transparency." Little did Bob know that this random thought would later provide entirely new possibilities for both the company and his career.

Jim Wellington was a damn good software engineer and systems designer. So good, the products he and his team created were always first rate and had never seen a problem until a year ago. In fact, Jim's brilliant mind and the success of his innovative designs made it easy to overlook some of his weaknesses on the management side of the business. Jim was the first to admit his own shortcomings. He always used to kid that he never started out to run a big company. He frequently called himself the accidental CEO.

"Ironic," Bob thought to himself, "I'm the new *Accidental CEO*."

The phone rang.

"Bob Harris," he answered as he automatically put the receiver to his ear.

"Bob, Phil Devine here. How about getting out of here for a while and getting some lunch?"

"Sounds good to me," said Bob. "I'll meet you at the elevator."

They walked up Monroe Street in silence and turned into the Golden Dragon. It was going to be Chinese. After the order was taken, Phil got right to the point.

"Bob, you're a go-to guy, but you've never been a CEO before. I know we told you we were going to initiate a search, but you've got history and a few of us on the Board think you've got what it takes to do the job, especially after your year in Europe. Your guys really like you in spite of working day and night to meet your deadlines. Would you be interested in the job full time?"

Bob just looked at Phil for a moment, surprised twice in as many hours. "Yes, I think I am," said Bob,

"Being the Senior Partner in a venture capital firm, I've had the opportunity to have this kind of conversation with chief executives more than a few times in since I founded DKM. So I have some input if you're open to hearing it, Bob. Are you?"

"Sure. That would be good," said Bob.

Phil took a moment to gather his thoughts.

"Before I founded DKM, I was CEO of Atlantic Communications for thirteen years, I don't know if you knew that?"

Bob shook his head indicating that he didn't.

"Well, I started Atlantic, just like Jim; and the damn thing grew up around me so fast, it was amazing. I can testify that nothing prepares you to be a CEO, Bob, absolutely nothing. As soon as you get the title, people begin to defer to you as though you know it all. And believe me, you don't. Because there's so much deference and there's so much to handle, you end up reacting rather than thinking things through.

"Jim was a great software engineer; we all know that. But he really had to stretch to handle being CEO. And it just about destroyed him.

"You're a sales and marketing guy, Bob. And while that experience will help in dealing with Wall Street, being CEO isn't just sales and marketing only faster; it's a hell of a lot more. You're getting a shot at the top spot because a few of us think you can do the job. But if you want to be considered for the job full time, you are going to have to convince three other Board members. To do that you need to be let in on some leadership secrets that aren't common knowledge these days, especially among new CEOs."

"What kind of secrets?" asked Bob.

Phil sat there for a few seconds.

"It's about context," said Phil. "And I don't want you to take what needs to be said out of context. So I want you to talk with a guy. His name is Jack Griffin. He's a former CEO himself who now works with other CEOs, especially CEOs in transition. I was introduced to him by one of my Board members when I decided to put Atlantic up for sale. What he did in just 90 days helped me add sixty million to the selling price. In fact, what I learned from Jack gave me the insight to start DKM. If you're open to it, I'll have him give you a call the first part of next week. Do yourself a favor and take his call."

"Okay, but I've got two questions."

"Sure," said Phil, sitting back in the booth.

"How the heck did Jack help you add $60 million to the sale of Atlantic in 90 days, and what does he know about CI that qualifies him to be able to help us?"

"Good questions, Bob." Phil sat forward and folded his hands on the table in front of him. He began, "First about Atlantic. We had grown like crazy but had been running ragged the last few years, pretty much like CI is now, except we were a hell of a lot bigger. I was tired and was ready to move on to something else.

Running a big company wasn't all that it was cracked up to be, at least not the way I was doing it at the time. Anyway, Jack helped me see that selling Atlantic was a good idea for me at the time *because running a big company wasn't what I loved to do*. And in that conversation he also showed me how some basic structural changes in the company could make it even more valuable. You see, people don't buy companies for the heck of it, they buy cash machines, but more importantly, they buy predictable cash machines. If I was to ever get free of the company I had to demonstrate that it could run without me. Jack helped us with the "predictable cash machine" part by helping us redefine the context of our business from being reactive to being creative. That's when I experienced how little I understood people. And understanding this shift from reactive to creative is why I want you to meet Jack."

Bob had some serious questions coming up in his mind but decided to stick with the original two questions.

"Okay, but what does he know about us?"

"Jack knows little about our current situation. I haven't spoken to him yet because I wanted to see if you'd be open to the idea first.

"What he can help you with doesn't require knowing the product or service. A good leader can run anything, no matter what terrain you drop him into. You should know that. Hell, you've been trained as a Marine. All the guns, tanks, jets, ships, missiles and strategy in the world are meaningless without good people and the ability to lead them.

"If you're going to sit in the CEO chair, Bob, you should know that the chair already has an agenda of its own. It's full of expectations. And if you're not clear what those expectations are, and if you don't know exactly who you are, and exactly what you want when you sit in it, well, the chair will run you. Instead of you running the company, the company will run you. Take a look at your people right now for example. Are they in charge, or is the next crisis in charge?"

After a short pause Phil continued, "Trust me, the CEO job can eat you alive. It's what happened to Jim. Hell, it's what happens to most of us when we first sit in the seat. And unfortunately, most of us don't understand what happened until its too late."

"What do you mean, it's what happened to Jim?" said Bob.

Phil was quiet for a few moments.

"Margie took the kids and moved back to Philadelphia last week. For Jim it was more than a wake-up call. He called me and the rest of the Board members on Wednesday and told us he wanted out. He said nothing was worth losing his family over. As you so well know, since going public, these last three years have been all consuming. It's been a virtual roller coaster. Yes, the company has been successful from an investment point of view, but the cost to Jim, especially with the Board and his family has been really high. Jim didn't know when to ask for help from the Board and he didn't know when to draw the line between work and family. Not unusual as it turns out, but still, it causes serious relationship issues. Both the Board and his family were trying to help him but he wouldn't let anyone in. He felt he had to do everything himself."

Bob had experienced Jim cutting people off before, both in meetings and through back channels. It was difficult to help Jim with anything once he made up his mind about something. But hey, Jim was the boss. That's just the way it is in business.

"Okay," said Bob, "tell Jack I'll take his call."

On the walk back to the office, they were both silent. Bob's mind was in hyper drive, ticking down the list of what he should do next. How his first staff meeting should unfold. How he should handle the Board. How he should handle Wall Street. How he could get everything under control.

"By the way, Bob" said Phil suddenly, "Jim wants you to call him as soon as you've had a chance to take all this in. He's sorry he dumped everything on you like this and wants to make the transition as smooth as possible. While his first priority is on saving his marriage, he doesn't intend to let this baby die either."

Phil knew there were other reasons for Jim leaving, but he and the Board had agreed that Jim would be the one to tell Bob the rest of the story.

"I understand," said Bob, even though he didn't understand at all. "I'll call Jim on Sunday after I've had a chance to review his projects. Rebecca has already given me the material, so I'll review it all by end of the day tomorrow. By the way Phil, I'm going to need your help as well."

"Whatever I can do, Bob," said Phil. "And make sure you talk with Jack soon."

CONSIDER

- The average CEO is smart, hard working and ambitious, but he or she rarely sets out to be CEO.

- In a seven year survey of over 300 CEOs, conducted by CEO^2, 97% of those interviewed stated that they had never expected to become a CEO – at least, not in that moment. They got their jobs by accident.

Imagine one day going into a Board of Directors meeting as the CFO and coming out as the CEO. It really happens. *"I couldn't believe it; they relieved John of his duties and pointed to me. 'George,' they said, 'we want you to serve as interim CEO while we do a search. That was over two years ago."*

Another CEO told us that all he had wanted to do was be a great programmer. Alan had some great applications he was exploring in the music industry when his brother-in-law shared what he was doing with a Venture Capitalist friend who just happened to be looking to exploit the recent trend in music distribution over the net. *"I went from extraordinary programmer to incompetent CEO in less than 24 hours. And the funny thing was, everyone treated me like I knew what I was doing – like the title alone would somehow give me what I needed to do the job. I'm talking investors as well as my employees here. I never set out to manage a company with 600 people but here I am. It's been quite an adventure, more than a little stressful, and at times very lonely."*

Still another CEO shared that his father, who founded a $200 million dollar electronic component and contract-manufacturing firm, suddenly died. Tom was working as a financial consultant for a top 5 accounting firm at the time and his mother asked him to step in for the family. *"During the first six months I looked at everything through a financial lens. It was my only experience so I fell back on it when I found myself in charge. I found out really fast that business is a heck of a lot more than the P&L. In fact the more time passed the more I found that 90% of the problems I ran into were people related. No one ever teaches you that, much less what to do about it. And many never find out about it until it's too late."*

Even CEOs brought into organizations as professional managers laughed when asked about their first jobs as CEOs. *"Until you asked I had completely forgotten about my first CEO assignment,"* said Steve, now Chairman and CEO of a billion dollar marketing firm based in NYC. *"After a few years it feels like you've always been in the job. Like you were born into it. The key to being CEO is much like being a consultant"* he said, *"your first order of business is to survive long enough to do some good. And you have a hell of a learning curve."*

- No matter how CEOs get their jobs, one thing is certain, there is not a lot of training for the job.

- The CEO chair has a compelling agenda of its own, regardless of who is sitting in it, especially if it's a public corporation.

- The chair will run the CEO if he or she is not well grounded in his or her own personal values and guiding principles. Ungrounded CEOs end up managing and reacting rather than leading and growing.

CHAPTER 4

TRANSITION

*We hardly notice those moments in time
that connect one part of our lives to the next.*

B ob finally phoned Jim, who was staying at his mother's house in Philadelphia, on Sunday evening. Jim was expecting the call but the first few moments were awkward nonetheless. After the initial hellos, Jim began.

"So this must be quite a surprise for you?"

"I think that's a fair statement," Bob retorted.

"Rebecca gave you my operations folders, yes?"

"Yes. I reviewed them over the weekend and they look pretty straightforward, except for the last folder. The one marked, 'The Surprise Factor.' What did you mean by that? There was nothing in it."

Jim didn't answer right away.

"There was too much to put in the folder, Bob. Or, maybe I should say that I didn't know how to articulate what needed to go in it. I suppose that's pretty lame for a former college professor. What I was working on...well, let me re-phrase that. The question I puzzled over for the last few years was, 'Why do the same problems come up over and over again?' Before the PDQ acquisition it was the same, of course. We still had the same stuff come up over and over again, but we were always able to handle things by working just a little harder and just a little longer. With PDQ we finally got overwhelmed and we didn't have enough hours in the day. You know how the staff meetings became. I'd talk and everyone else just sat there or there would be the occasional shouting match. I'd tell everyone what I expected, but nothing was happening. I felt like the kid with all his fingers plugging holes in the dike."

There was a pause in the conversation, as each man struggled with his thoughts. Bob remembered the meetings the way Jim was describing them, but with a different spin. There was a lot of silence in the meetings because Jim thought he had all the answers. He had to be right. As a result, few would speak up if they had a difference of opinion. And on those rare occasions when someone would disagree or offer a different opinion, Jim would be compelled to demonstrate why the other the person was wrong and why Jim's course was right. Bob wouldn't deny that Jim was smart as hell, but so were his direct reports. While Bob was out of the country the meetings had shifted to a pattern of grin and bear it between Jim and senior staff. People either shut up or there would be a disagreement followed by a lecture.

As if that weren't enough, confrontation escalated when PDQ was acquired and two of their senior guys joined the senior staff. Winning through attack and intimidation became commonplace. While CI's culture was for the most part, 'grin and bear it,' PDQ's turned out to be 'rip and tear it'. Why hadn't we seen this before the deal?

Jim interrupted Bob's unspoken memories. "Looking back, it was like PDQ was the straw that broke the camel's back. Before we acquired them, we were already running flat out, but at the time I thought the acquisition would help solve our growing throughput issues and save us time to market in development of our 6.0 release.

"Sort of like a couple having a baby to save the marriage," Jim mused. "In the end it didn't help the company and certainly didn't help my marriage."

The line went quiet again.

"Jim, are you still there?" said Bob into the silence.

"Yes. I guess I was dragged back to why we're having this conversation, Bob – to why you're the CEO and I'm not. Listen, we have a great product with great people. But the company can't sustain the pace at which we've been driving ourselves. I've even overheard some of the guys calling it a death march; and the sad part is, I know what they mean. I just didn't know what to do to shake us out of the situation. Before PDQ we were already expanding like crazy and our systems and processes were being held together with string and bailing wire. I hoped the quality program would have helped us there but it was too little too late. Since acquiring PDQ we've had four rounds of lay offs because of the integration effort and the people who are left are frightened they might be next. Our management team is fragmented, defensive and polarized. And the hours are brutal and people are tired," he concluded.

Bob agreed and began thinking to himself, "It's true. Over the past year, the cohesiveness of the senior team changed quite a bit. Jim never integrated the PDQ staff to create a new team. Bob remembered Jim saying it was like herding cats with seven strong managers trying to protect their own turf." Aloud, Bob said "Well what can you do, Jim, especially since the economy's gone to hell?"

"The Surprise Factor, Bob. Solve that and you sustain and grow the company."

After another pause, Jim continued. "I had some ideas to address all of this, but I was too busy putting out fires to even think about how to implement them."

"What kind of ideas, Jim? And tell me more about the surprise factor. What are you talking about exactly, because I'm a little lost here," said Bob with some irritation.

"Well, number one, if we all go to work to do a good job – and I believe we do – and we've got good people, then why do we all spend so much time putting out fires and doing the same things over and over? What's missing that would make the difference? We all know how to be individual heroes, but none of us seems to know how to work as a team. In a candid moment last year Doug Martin in HR told me it was because the executive staff is made up of such highly dominant personalities, and each of us knows *the* way. The result is we end up pulling the company in a bunch of different directions. And last year, you remember the Total Quality Initiative we instituted? Hell, we spent over two hundred grand, and what do we have to show for it? I thought it would make a difference in helping us focus and work on the right things, but somehow we keep being yanked into the day-to-day without changing anything of consequence. When was the last time you saw anyone present a completed project that made a contribution to how we do business?"

Privately, Bob thought he knew what would fix things. Jim tried to operate things too much by committees that had no authority. Bob felt more chain of command was needed.

"You're right, Jim," Bob said aloud, "we just can't sustain the kind of pace we've been running without changing something. Sooner or later the system will break."

"Bob, the system's already broke." said Jim with some urgency. "And while the Board's being kind to me in public, the truth of the matter is, I was being asked to leave by three of the five Board members."

"What, how the hell could they do that?" Bob countered, incredulous.

"Phil Devine and Chris Plumber wanted to give me more time. But with Margie not just threatening, but actually leaving, I just didn't have the stomach to fight the Board. I just ran out of fingers for the dyke and, well, Bob, I'm not kidding, I never wanted to be a CEO to begin with. In many ways, it's a big relief."

Bob was surprised and angry that Jim could be dismissed from his own company so easily. He was also a little miffed at Jim's "being relieved" comment. Now he was holding the bag. But he put his feelings aside and the two men continued for another hour reviewing every aspect of the business. In spite of the seriousness of their conversation, they couldn't help but reminisce and laugh about the early days.

Bob was especially disappointed at the condition of the domestic sales pipeline, which Jim also reported as dismal. In addition, Development's performance was just as bad with severe throughput issues.

As they were concluding their discussion, Bob asked, "So what do you know about a guy named Jack Griffin? Phil wants me to talk to him"

Jim was silent for a few minutes.

"I guess I felt a little pissed off when Phil asked me to talk with Griffin a few years back. After all, what did I need some coach telling me what to do? Looking at it now I guess my ego just got the best of me. I took a pass and decided to go with the Quality Initiative instead. In hindsight I should have at least talked to the guy if for no other reason than to get a reality check. Phil never mentioned it again after I told him I wanted to do the quality program. But if Phil wants you to talk with him I'd suggest you do. It can't hurt. Your year in Europe gave you some new experiences. But, I can tell you, Bob, nothing prepares you to be a CEO."

"That's what Phil said."

"Well then, that makes two of us. Make sure you talk with him sooner rather than later," said Jim rather forcefully.

"Alright," said Bob. "Things will be crazy all next week so I might as well talk to him before it becomes impossible."

After hanging up with Jim, Bob took some time to finalize his notes about his conversation with Jim before he called his wife, Linda. He saw that he had circled over and over again *"The Surprise Factor."*

CALLING HOME

Bob shared the situation with his wife Linda over the phone. She was, as she had always been in their relationship, supportive and excited for Bob. But after the initial euphoria, they began to look at how Bob's new responsibilities would affect their lives. In his new role as acting CEO, they both realized that he would be away from home a lot more than he had in the recent past, at least in the beginning. Since moving to London, Bob's travel schedule was dramatically reduced from when they were in the States and they had begun to really enjoy their time together, especially their weekend jaunts with the children to Paris and Rome. And while Linda was proud that Bob had been entrusted with the company, she wasn't sure how she felt about losing him to the expanded role of CEO. Especially after what happened between Margie and Jim.

Linda and Margie had become best friends over the years and Linda knew how much Margie had come to resent the company. She recalled one of their conversations. "Jim keeps telling me he's doing it all for us," Margie had shared with Linda just a few months before. "Well he's not doing it for us; he's doing it for himself. He's being totally selfish and I don't know how much longer I can take it. He's hardly ever home and when he is, he spends most of his time on the phone or in his office answering e-mails," she had said. Linda shared the conversation and her concerns with Bob but he protested that this was an amazing opportunity for them and the sacrifice now would give them more time together later. Linda wasn't so sure.

They both realized that neither one of them knew the real meaning of this sudden change in their lives, or how it would affect them, but they both agreed to give it a chance. Given the CEO job could be temporary, Linda thought it best to remain in London until their children, Jeremy and Jenny, finished out the school year. Bob agreed. That would give Bob five months to do whatever he had to do to make the job work for the company, and for the family. They talked off and on throughout the weekend as new issues arose. What about the logistics? How often would he get home? What would they tell the children?

Monday came too quickly. On the drive to the office Bob's mind was again filled with a thousand questions. However, within a few minutes, he brought himself into focus with a single directive: "Don't let it get away from you like Jim did. *Take control!*"

CONSIDER

- **The Surprise Factor** – Seemingly invisible forces; destabilizing factors; people not communicating; seemingly simple things falling through the cracks; thoughtlessness; being surprised by employee and manager behavior; covering up; holding information close to the vest; not trusting one another; offense being taken when none is intended; important issues being ignored; not taking the time to plan; not knowing how to plan; the elephant in the room; tolerating the elephant in the room; misunderstandings; making up stories; spreading gossip; malicious compliance; judging one another unfairly; pigeon-holing one another; not liking one another; being afraid to ask or question or contribute; not hearing what's really being said; focusing on what's wrong; lack of appreciation; intimidating behavior; being closed to new ideas; being addicted to looking good at all costs; passing the buck; lack of follow-through.

- What if you were able to recognize and neutralize the surprise factor in your organization? What would that be worth in terms of productivity and morale?

CHAPTER 5

THE CONSULTANT'S FIRST CALL

"The soft stuff actually is the hard stuff."
— Carly Fiorina, former CEO, Hewlett-Packard

As Bob walked into his office at 6:30 A.M. his phone was already ringing. He was the first one in and he hurried to catch the call, although he couldn't imagine who would be calling this early.

"Hi, Bob, this is Jack Griffin. Phil said you'd be expecting my call. Do you have a few minutes to talk now?"

"Sure, Jack, but let's make it quick because I'm still preparing for my first staff meeting. Boy, you must be up early. I thought you were in California?

"Actually I'm working in New York this week and just thought I'd take a chance on getting you while I'm on a break," admitted Jack.

"So, I understand you work with CEOs. How do you do that?"

"Very carefully!" said Jack. The two men laughed. "Seriously, though, I help CEOs and their people get what they want out of their lives and their work."

"Hmm, listen, Jack, this sounds like soft stuff to me. I know that Phil recommended that we talk, but I don't have a lot of time for soft stuff right now. Besides, I've never seen any of it last more than a few weeks."

"I understand," said Jack.

"What I want to do is drive this company forward and do it now. How can you help me do that? Phil said you had some CEO secrets I need to learn, so give me a couple of secrets and let me try them out." Although Bob made his request in a somewhat joking manner, he was more than half serious.

Jack quietly smiled to himself on the other end of the line and then responded. "I suppose I could do that, but any suggestions I could give you now would be out of context and would be of no help to you in any meaningful way. Look, Bob, I can see that your mind is somewhere else, so why don't we take this up another time when you get your feet under you. And besides, in my experience, driving too hard for results can be both unproductive and exhausting."

Bob found himself getting a little irritated with this kind of talk. "Listen Jack, I've been a consultant for two of the Big 5. I know all about best practices and …"

"Bob," said Jack abruptly, "the Big 5 is now the Big 4. And it used to be the Big 8. Things change. What you did yesterday won't necessarily get you a better tomorrow. How would you like to be able to *design the future rather than just react to it?* How would you like to be able *to intend for something to happen and actually have it happen?*"

"What are you, some kind of wizard?" Bob asked sarcastically.

Jack smiled again as he realized he had already managed to rub Bob the wrong way. This was not a new phenomenon, of course, so he just continued to smile and kept quiet on the other end of the line.

Bob didn't know why he was so ticked. Yet at the same time, something that Jack had said touched him, "…design the future rather than just react to it…intend something and have it happen." Jack's words somehow felt familiar to him, very real and appealing. Yeah, right, like the desire to be able to fly, he thought. Silly. That put a smile on his face and he laughed at himself and immediately calmed down. Finally, he picked up the conversation.

"Listen, Jack, like I said, I have to finish preparing for this meeting. Let me think about this a little. Phil speaks very highly of you, but I want to be clear about what I need from you before we continue this conversation. And, I'm not sure what that is yet. Why don't you give me a call the beginning of next week?"

"Fair enough, when would be a good time to call?" said Jack.

"Call me at the Chicago number on Tuesday morning, a week from tomorrow, before 10 A.M. your time. That's noon here."

"That's good for me as well. I'll talk to you then," said Jack.

"And Jack," Bob closed, "if I don't answer the phone, page my assistant Rebecca. She'll track me down."

"Thanks," said Jack, "I appreciate that."

"Perhaps I didn't piss Bob off as much as I thought," Jack mused. "Maybe this guy *has* got what it takes."

Bob didn't like Jack's smart-ass remark, "The Big 5 is now the Big 4, things change!" But he felt Jack was right about one thing. All the good things Jim might have done in the past just don't seem to matter right now. The Board is looking for something new. "Stop the bleeding and build a new foundation." Bob rubbed his eyes. The image of the *"Surprise Factor"* circled in his notes momentarily flashed by.

Bob thought to himself, "The last quarter's revenue looked good. We haven't missed making our numbers since we went public. I'd better talk with Neil Coulter, and soon."

CONSIDER

- Why is it once someone becomes the boss, people stop questioning them? Silly question, really. We're afraid and at the same time, why should we think if they've got all the answers?

- The soft stuff *is* the hard stuff. But great leaders have always known that.

- Driving a company kills it, wears it out.

- Inspiring a company grows it, lights it up.

- How would you like to design the future rather than just react to it?

- How would you like to intend something and actually have it happen?

CHAPTER 6

BEING CEO

"It is a lonely job."
— Patricia Russo, CEO, Lucent Technologies

Right after his phone call with Jack, Bob realized he needed some coffee. He went into the small kitchen next to his office, found the necessary supplies and got a pot brewing. When Rebecca came in it was ready and Jack poured a cup for her.

Rebecca was surprised by the gesture and thought to herself, "I'm beginning to like this guy already."

Bob set up camp on the conference table in Jim's office. He and Rebecca got right to work and went through each folder and mapped out a meeting agenda that was geared to asking questions and listening. There were more than a few questions Bob had about the apparent lack of success in integrating the two companies, especially the two development groups. Jim had decided to keep the PDQ development group in Portland, Oregon and not move it to Chicago, thinking it would be a good test of the company's growing philosophy of managing with dispersed teams and its new remote internet architecture.

"There's a lot of firefighting, but what's new with that?" thought Bob. "Isn't this just the way things are in a high tech company on the bleeding edge?"

Both CI and PDQ specialized in developing software applications to assist their customers in managing mission critical projects throughout distributed organizations. Now that CI was becoming even more distributed itself, Bob wrote a note to ask Chris Cooper how the software integration was going and which version they were using to manage their own mission critical projects. He would later find out that few in either PDQ or CI were using CI software.

"So how do you see this meeting going?" Rebecca asked.

"All I know so far is the reason Jim decided to step down. The projects Jim was working on all seem pretty straightforward to me," said Bob, "except the last one, of course. I spoke with Jim about it over the weekend but was wondering if you had any additional insight into the last folder. Do you know what he meant by that one?" Bob spread the folders out in front of Rebecca.

1. Integrating PDQ
2. New accounts and expanding existing customer penetration
3. Upgrading staff
4. Engineering reliability of release 6.0
5. Leveraging the Board
6. The Surprise Factor

"Sort of," said Rebecca. "The last folder refers to the problems with the other five. I know Jim was agitated about how things continue to be in crisis, even after all these years of success, and despite recruiting all the new people from larger organizations and acquiring PDQ's assets. I guess you can say it was a good strategy badly executed. We all hoped the new talent would bring more order to things, but the new guys seem to be floundering as badly as everyone else. And I know that Jim thought Chris Cooper would integrate the Development effort faster. Bumpy road there." she said.

"Can you expand on that?" Bob asked.

"Well, as you know, Chris Cooper and Bill Peters came when we bought PDQ. Everyone thought they had something we didn't." Rebecca's face and tone of voice told the truth about how she was feeling. "And Doug Martin, Nancy Cummings, Neil Coulter and Mike Clark are all former Oracle people. They were all supposedly very successful in their previous jobs, but have struggled with how little structure and resources we have here."

"Hmmm," mused Bob to himself, "I can see why Jim referred to Rebecca as a pistol. She definitely has some insight and is not afraid to express her opinions."

"Jim loved the fast pace," she continued, "but he said on more than one occasion that there was never enough time to do anything right, but always enough time to do it over. I guess he never found an answer to that dilemma."

"I can understand his decision to leave at some level," said Bob. "But understanding his decision doesn't at all answer the question about what's next. I'll bet the staff is waiting for another shoe to drop. What do you think?"

"Is there another shoe?" asked Rebecca.

Bob knew there was, but replied, "Well, I guess we'll find out together. Are you ready to go in?"

"Sure, I'll see you in there," Rebecca answered, heading into the Board room to handle last-minute details.

Bob sat there for a few minutes and thought about Rebecca's last question. Oh well, handling dropping shoes is what he'd been trained for his entire life. No big deal. He could handle it.

Just then Neil Coulter, the CFO, stuck his head in the door. "Hello, Bob. I was wondering if we could have a moment before the staff meeting. I have some things you might want to know about before you go in."

"Yes, absolutely Neil, just the person I wanted to see. Come on in. I've had my hands full getting up to speed and missed you on Friday, but God knows I can't function without your input. I'd like to have a more in-depth discussion before the end of the day, but for right now I'd like your take on Phil's comment the other day. You know, the 'stop the bleeding and build a new foundation' one."

"Well, Phil was right. We are bleeding. Revenue was strong through last quarter because, believe it or not, we were still operating from what was already in the pipeline before you left, but then sales took a nosedive at the beginning of this quarter and the pipeline looks pretty weak for the foreseeable future. I mean the pipeline sucks. In fact Nancy has made up much of the short fall by expanding service contracts and existing customer programs. I know you like the guy you brought in from PDQ to replace you in sales leadership..."

"Bill Peters, yeah, he seemed to be perfect for the job, but I didn't get much support from him while I was in Europe," said

Bob.

"Well, he hasn't been anywhere near as effective as we all thought he would be. Hell, as you know, he fired all but one of *our* people and brought in most of his own people. While things may still turn out, Bob, we've got nothing in the pipeline that I can see. The lack of sales, coupled with letting a lot of CI's development old timers go makes it look like we have no confidence in the people who got us here in the first place.

"The real issue you're going to be facing in there is no one is working together. Acquiring PDQ only made the lack of teamwork worse. I'm beginning to think that we're not going to get what we paid for out of these guys. And to make things worse, the integration costs are way beyond what we projected."

Letting that sink in for a moment, Neil said, "I can't tell you, Bob, how letting so many of the original CI guys go in the acquisition, especially so many from development, hurt us on the morale front. All the trust is gone. We've got a lot of rebuilding to do"

The two men looked at one another supportively.

"Thanks, Neil. I have to admit I was surprised that Bill laid off all my people, but I had my hands too full to look into it and I didn't want appear to second-guess the guy. I was able to help a couple of my people who were axed, but it was a rough transition for the rest of them. They all felt betrayed."

After a short pause, Bob stood up, signaling an end to the meeting and said, "I don't know what this morning's meeting will bring; but regardless, let's get together later today – can you make an early dinner tonight?"

"No problem. I've got all the financials ready. Do you want to review them first?" offered Neil.

"No, I'd rather you take me through them," replied Bob.

"Okay, will do," said Neil, who was already up and headed out the door.

"Yup," said Bob to himself, already deep in thought, "So much for the next shoe! Hell, it's going to be raining shoes!"

THE FIRST STAFF MEETING

When Bob walked into the meeting, he was quick to notice that everyone was there. Quite a feat considering Dave Finney, V.P. of Applications Engineering had been working with clients in Hong Kong just a few days ago. He had to have caught the red eye to get here. And Nancy Cummings, V.P. of Professional Services, cut her vacation in the Bahamas short. Chris Cooper, V.P. Development, came in from Portland, Bill Peters, the new V.P. of Domestic Sales & Marketing from Los Angeles and Mike Clark, V.P. of Engineering and IT from Cincinnati, and of course Neil Coulter, the CFO and Rebecca. As he scanned the room again he noticed that Doug Martin, the Director of HR, wasn't in the room. Bob was surprised that Neil hadn't asked him to attend. Bob made a mental note to speak with Doug separately about how this was all being addressed with the employees. He realized he should have done it earlier. Oh well.

Bob launched right into it.

"Thank you all for being here. I wish the circumstances were different, but I expect we will handle things the way we always have. Let's open it up for questions or comments. Does anyone have anything to say about our situation?"

There was a lot of looking around but no one seemed to have anything to say. Dave Finney, VP of Applications Engineering was the first to speak up.

"What is 'spending more time with the family' supposed to tell us about why Jim decided to leave? I don't get it. Jim was just as driven as ever up until the Friday surprise. What happened? Why all of a sudden? Why now?"

With that comment there was a flurry of conversation and speculation. Bob waited until the commotion died down and the attention again focused on him. He began to share what he had learned from his conversations with Phil and then Jim over the weekend – leaving out the fact that Jim was being asked to leave.

"I don't have to tell any of you that this is all confidential. None of this leaves the room."

Heads nodded in agreement.

"Spending time with his family is necessary right now," said Bob. "When I spoke with Jim last night he was pretty determined to turn his marriage around. He had been, as you just said Dave, driven for the past few years. So much so that he had neglected his family and didn't even notice anything was wrong. He said he had taken his family for granted and this was one wake up call he wasn't going to ignore. His family needs him right now. So that's what he decided to do, and you all know how single minded he can be."

Bob paused for a minute. "Jim is from Philadelphia, and that's where he is now and where he will be for the foreseeable future."

Bob let that sink in for a few seconds, and then continued, "Jim wanted us to know that he believes in our collective ability to drive the company forward. The Board, with Jim's approval, has asked me to be the interim CEO while they do a search for a permanent replacement. I've accepted the interim job and look forward to working with each of you. And, I might as well let you know, I am in the running for the permanent job as well."

Bob looked around the room to a poker-faced crowd, then advanced, "As you might imagine, I am going to need some time to get to know what's going on. I've been focused on European sales and marketing and, as Phil Knight reminded me on Friday, being good at sales and marketing doesn't prepare you to be a good CEO. I'd like to schedule an hour with each of you to go over where you are right now and any issues or opportunities you want me to be aware of. I will be available for more in-depth conversations in the days ahead. But right now I need to know the critical issues."

Conversation erupted again, but this time it was led by some remarks from Chris Cooper, the Senior VP of Software Development, – and a co-founder of PDQ – about how sales would never say 'no' to a customer. "I've got so many requests for changes it's ridiculous. Why can't you guys sell what you've got?" continued Chris. After thirty minutes of allowing defense of their respective departments, which Bob found very instructive in and of itself – he brought the focus of the meeting back to the table.

"I had two objectives for today's meeting. The first was to

discuss Jim's leaving and what that means for the future of the company and second, to get a handle on the key issues we are facing. It's clear that we're collectively not happy about Jim's choice, but that's not going to change. It's also clear that we have some work to do to get the company working as a team," said Bob with some disappointment in his voice. The meeting calmed down markedly.

"At this point, I'd like to begin our individual meetings. Nancy, Dave, I want to see you guys first," said Bob as he stood and gathered his notes, "because you traveled the furthest, and I know you want to get back in the field. The rest of you, let's get together beginning first thing tomorrow. Chris, I know that will require you to stay over. Can you arrange it?"

"Not a problem," said Chris.

"Schedule with Rebecca before you leave this morning. Now, before we move on, are there any burning issues that need to be put on the table right now that just can't wait?" Bob asked.

Again, a lot of looking at one another but this time no one said anything. Bob thought about Jim's comment the night before about no one speaking up in meetings when he asked for input.

"Good, I'll look forward to speaking with each of you. Nancy, do you mind being first so we can get you back to your vacation?"

"Thanks, Bob," said Nancy, "I'm as prepared as I'll ever be, I suppose."

The meeting ended in silence as each headed for the door.

Nancy and Bob walked into Jim's office. Bob realized it would remain Jim's office for some time to come. In a conscious effort to create an informal setting, Bob moved to the round conference table rather than the desk where they took seats opposite one another.

ONE-ON-ONES

PROFESSIONAL SERVICES – NANCY CUMMINGS

"Well, Nancy, you're the first. What should I know in order to help all of us to go forward?"

Nancy and Bob had known each other for about a year and a half, meeting six months before he was reassigned to Europe, but they were not very close. She was one of the new breed that Jim and the Board spoke about so often, someone with the confidence of having "been there and done that." Nancy had come from a stellar career with IBM Global Services and most recently from Oracle. Challenges or setbacks didn't seem to faze her. She understood getting the job done without excuses. Never mind if there were some dead bodies along the way. If things got stuck, she would drive over, around or through the obstacles.

As VP of Professional Services, her department teamed with Marketing and Sales to make clean installations, explore new opportunities with customers and turn those new ideas into additional revenue. Lately she wasn't able to fulfill quotas as quickly as she had in the past. Because of Chris's constant lobbying, she had seen more and more of her engineering resources transferred to PDQ, and getting them to follow through on updates and new applications was turning into a nightmare. That had caused more than a little stress between her department and Development, not to mention Quality and IT. She was working hard at putting out the fires that were erupting all around her and was beginning to feel attacked by some of her peers. She recently heard through the grapevine that Chris had called for her replacement on a few occasions with Jim, although Jim never mentioned it to her. She wasn't too eager to say anything about that in this meeting.

"Congratulations on the new job," said Nancy. "How are you feeling about the promotion and where do you think we'll go from here?" she said, guiding the conversation away from what she was really thinking.

"Well I've talked with my wife, Linda, over the weekend so I guess you can say I'm ready for whatever and however long it takes to be successful. So the short version is I'm looking forward to the challenge. Nancy, what I need from you and the rest of the senior staff is an early warning system so I don't get blindsided by problems. So what should I know that you don't really want to tell me?" Bob kidded.

Nancy hesitated.

"I'd like to think about that a little. I don't want to sound like a complainer."

"Feel free to speak your mind, Nancy," said Bob, "we'll just call it thinking out loud."

Nancy took a deep breath and started. "Okay, Bob. I've had a growing concern about our ability to deliver on our new applications, much less updates and custom work, and I'm still trying to find out exactly what's getting in the way."

"Can you give me an example?" asked Bob.

"To be specific, for the past six months, especially since Development has been shifted to PDQ in Portland, new applications never have a completion date assigned to them, much less an implementation date. The GE job, for example, has been lost in a black hole for over six weeks now and I can't get anyone at PDQ, excuse me, I mean in Development, to tell me where it is," Nancy said.

Bob noted the reference to PDQ as a separate entity. It wasn't the first time he'd heard this slip, but he was going to make it among the last.

"Every time I call Development I'm told they're working on the GE job but I'm given no time frame or who the project is assigned to. GE is okay with it for now because their application slipped a few months – highly unusual for them. However, their project manager, Mike Cramer – you met him last month in Toronto at the trade show – well he asked me about the delay twice this week," Nancy confided. "On top of that, our last two updates required an inordinate amount of work just to get up and running, and all the bugs aren't out of them yet. My people are getting a little gun-shy about promising our customers delivery dates. You know what missed deadlines can do to our pipeline and our Professional Services Group revenue stream. And with sales revenue slowing up, I know that you're going to be depending on me to increase existing client license revenue to cover the shortfall. I can't do that if I don't know project status, and no one's telling me anything these days."

"Well, in fairness, we're still trying to swallow PDQ and have shifted a lot of our resources around, so, I guess it's reasonable to assume a fix is in the works. Keep me informed, and let me know if you need a push from my end," said Bob.

"Yeah, right," thought Nancy to herself, "just more lip service, but no real answers to the question of how I can get the information I need."

Meanwhile, Bob added another note to his list to check if a fix really was coming down the pike. "Never want to assume something as important as that," he thought.

During the remainder of the hour they reviewed field installation schedules and the revenue pipeline for the next quarter. Nancy's drive and attitude began to give Bob more confidence that she would handle whatever came her way. But he sensed something was still being held back. Oh well, everything seemed to be okay enough. Proceed with caution.

APPLICATIONS – DAVE FINNEY

A few minutes after Nancy left, Dave Finney came in. As VP of Applications Engineering, he was responsible for designing specialty applications for the largest clients. Dave had been with CI from the first year and Bob knew him to be a solid engineer and manager whose people highly respected and liked him. He has always been a reliable guy who never let you down, but that had begun to change.

"I'm beginning to feel like the company looks at us as an inconvenience, Bob. My people code the new applications Nancy and her group design, but Chris's Development group in Portland is responsible for integrating them into the next release. These days no one seems to have a handle on exactly what or when the next release is going to be. I was just told that two integration apps critical to G.E. aren't even being considered for inclusion. That's a lot of revenue being put at risk. And when I questioned Chris about it, he told me that he wasn't going to be held hostage by any client. I don't like that attitude one damn bit." Dave said with some urgency.

Neither did Bob.

CFO/FINANCE – NEIL COULTER

The meeting with Neil Coulter later that day went well. Neil was the kind of deliberately strategic thinker you want on your team, especially when the shit hits the fan. A product of the big accounting and consulting firms, Neil had seen it all, and was convinced he knew it all as well. Jim had told Bob that Neil had saved his ass on more than a few occasions and would make a great CEO himself if he could just curb his temper. You never knew when Neil would go off. Regardless, Bob was glad to have him at his side. He knew Neil only got pissed when someone did something really stupid. Unfortunately, most things people did appeared stupid to Neil. But at least he had an equal opportunity temper. It didn't matter who you were, if you did something he considered really stupid, title meant nothing at all to Neil, as both Jim and Bob could testify. But in spite of his gruff exterior, Neil cared about the company and really wanted people to be successful. His way of showing his caring side left something to be desired, however. So Bob was surprised when Neil closed the very productive financial meeting with, "If you sing the song and create a little harmony around here Bob, I'll keep the cash flowing for you." Bob knew he would, and ended the meeting with a smile on his face. "Oh, Neil, do you mind if I talk with Doug Martin for a bit. I want to get his perspective on the effect this is having on the employees. You're welcome to sit in."

"Not a problem," said Neil, "why don't you spend the time with Doug and if you need me for anything you can give me a buzz." Bob appreciated that and had Rebecca schedule Doug for two o'clock the next day.

PRODUCT DEVELOPMENT – CHRIS COOPER

The next morning Bob met Chris Cooper, PDQ's co-founder and currently CI's Senior VP of Development.

It occurred to Bob that he hadn't, until this very minute, considered how Chris might feel about being passed over for the CEO slot. Come to think of it, Phil hadn't mentioned how the selection process took place, and Bob hadn't asked. It had all happened so fast. He added to his mental list, "Why not Chris?"

The meeting started out casually enough with the two men getting some coffee. Chris's cell phone rang. Chris apologized to Bob, but said he had to take the call. Chris wasn't long but his demeanor and language on the call were really out of line. Bob felt Chris's language and cynical attitude was borderline abusive to whomever was on the other end of the line.

"Sorry," said Chris, once he was off the phone. "I've been jacked around so many times this month that I just can't take it anymore. I've had to shift my team's focus four times in the last ten days to satisfy the latest crisis from Applications and Global Support. If it isn't a firefight from Nancy's group to contend with, then it's Sales & Marketing constantly changing their specifications for the next software release. We have finite resources, Bob, and being in a Product Development meeting lately has felt like moving chairs on the Titanic. All I do is spend my time re-allocating resources to projects that continue to keep us from getting 6.0 out the door. Why can't we sell what we already have? Why does an application have so many damn changes and why can't Marketing get their shit together and give me a spec they're willing to live with?"

Chris saw the expression on Bob's face harden.

"Look, I'm sorry Bob. But when I agreed to take over Development I had no idea CI's development process flow was so screwed up. In order to fix it, I can't afford to fight with Sales, Applications and Marketing at the same time. These last nine months have been hell. I don't know how much longer we can do this death-march crap. People keep burning out. I've had Phil Dunlap and Judy Carp resign in the last two days. People need a life that's more than spinning their wheels 24/7."

"So what are you saying, Chris?" Bob prompted.

"I think Nancy Cummings and Dave Finney are weak. You should probably replace both of them. And I'm saying that I should handle Applications Engineering as part of Development," stated Chris flatly.

Bob was really alarmed at what this guy was saying and answered his own question about *why not Chris?* Chris's department, by his own admission, was in shambles, and he's blaming others for it. Who do I believe, Nancy, Dave or him?

Bob's direct reports didn't like each other, and were blaming each other for the problems in Development and Sales. "It looks like our integration effort failed to take egos and personalities into consideration," Bob thought.

They spoke for a few minutes longer, but everything Chris said was negative and the only way to fix it was to either fire someone or let him take over the department. Bob was not at all happy with the conversation. If it were up to Chris he would run everything. "Hum," thought Bob, "I guess I know how Chris must feel about working for me – the lowly sales guy from Europe."

SALES & MARKETING – BILL PETERS

Since his meeting with Chris was shorter than Bob had scheduled, he called Bill Peters to join him for an early lunch. Fortunately, Bill was able to make it so within ten minutes they were heading out of the building. This was their first one-on-one meeting since Bob handed Bill the reins to Sales and Marketing a year ago.

Bill was not looking forward to the meeting because sales were not living up to forecast and he didn't know when it was going to change.

Bob waved a cab down and asked the driver to take them to an out of the way restaurant so they could have some privacy. Bob knew it could be a tense meeting. When they got to the restaurant Bob started the conversation after they had ordered by asking as pleasantly as he could. "Well, what's going on Bill?" Considering that Bob was still upset by Chris's abusive behavior, it was quite an effort to be cordial and to assume an air of neutrality.

Bill misread Bob's tone, thinking it to be patronizing. He folded his hands in front of him and looked down at his napkin. "I wish I could give you better news, Bob, but I can't. So all I can do is take responsibility for the situation. Would you like me to resign?"

That was the second time a key staff member had been ready to fall on their sword for the organization, Rebecca being the first. Bob felt better about Bill because he so readily took responsibility. "That's not what I had in mind, Bill," said Bob, reaching for his Diet Coke the waiter had just placed on the table. "Since we find ourselves in a new situation, why don't we begin by catching up."

Bill leaned back in his chair and looked at Bob for a moment. Clearly he wasn't going to be fired today.

HUMAN RESOURCES – DOUG MARTIN

Because of a few firefights in Europe, two o'clock came and went and it wasn't until four forty-five when Bob was finally able to meet with Doug Martin. Bob was sensitive to having put off the meeting earlier because Jim had never given much sway to HR. He treated the department like a necessary evil and rarely asked advice or input from them regarding hiring, development or advancement issues. But if Bob was to change things, he felt he needed to include Doug.

"Hi Doug, thanks for making the time," said Bob as he got up from his desk, took off his headset and extended his hand. "I'm really sorry about the delay."

As the two men shook hands, Doug said, "Well, I'm here now, so how can I help?"

Bob guided Doug to the conference table and motioned for him to take a seat. He walked over to the small refrigerator and asked, "Can I get you anything?"

"Got any Diet Dr. Pepper?"

Bob took a look, "Yes, we do." Bob took two cans out and moved toward the conference table. "In the can okay? "

"Great," said Doug, who took the soda, popped the top and took a long swallow.

The two men sat for a moment.

"Doug, I need your help. I am planning to do something that we've never done before and I need someone who can help me follow through."

"What do you mean?"

Bob smiled, and then looked down for a moment, collecting his thoughts. Doug took another sip of his soda and waited.

"I'm still figuring out what I mean. But you can help me a great deal by telling me, from your perspective, how people are feeling – about the company and Jim's leaving."

"Pardon me?" said Doug, actually turning a little red, not quite sure what to make of this. "I don't know what you mean. What can I tell you?"

"I don't know, maybe nothing, maybe everything. I want your view of things. How are the people holding up? What are the key issues from your perspective as the Director of Human Resources?"

"You mean the Director of Compliance, don't you?

This time it was Bob who said, "Pardon me?"

"Listen, Bob, I really liked this job when I first came here three years ago. I was hired as the Director of HR with the promise that I could have a hand in developing our people and the organization. But aside from the Quality initiative, which I really had little to do with, we haven't spent much at all in developing our people. People just show up and are expected to know what to do. In my experience, they don't. They just bring their old baggage from their previous company and try to install it here. I just finished my Masters degree this year in Human Development, Bob, and in comparison to what we could be doing here; we are acting like a bunch of Neanderthals."

Bob actually laughed at the comment. "Go on," he encouraged Doug, "tell me how your really feel!"

"I don't know if you would want to look at them, but here are three proposals that I gave Jim over the past three years to improve morale, help with the integration and engage and develop our people," said Doug as he slid them across the table toward Bob. "Each time my request for these programs was denied because of lack of budget. Even simple organizational surveys were denied. And then, all of a sudden we're spending two hundred and fifty thousand dollars on a quality program to have outsiders come in and tell us how to run our business. It really pissed everyone off."

"And where are you in all of this?" asked Bob.

"Well, to tell you the truth, Bob, I have an offer and plan on leaving in two weeks. I just told Neil this morning. And unfortunately, I don't think I'm the only one. That's what I thought this conversation was going to be about. I never had many one-on-one's with Jim so it was a surprise when Neil said you wanted to see me after his meeting with you yesterday."

That surprised Bob. They both sat there sipping on their drinks.

"I'm sorry to hear that, Doug. Your deciding to leave, I mean. Is there anything I can do to change your mind?"

"I don't know. What do you have in mind?"

"I'm not sure. A few days ago I was a sales guy in Europe and today I'm acting CEO. If I had the answers we probably wouldn't be having this conversation. But somehow I just have the feeling that we haven't been leveraging what we already have. We certainly haven't been leveraging your training and experience!"

Doug began to feel listened to for the first time since he came to work at the company. "So what does that mean?" he asked.

"Well, Doug, I'm going into the field to listen to our people over the next few weeks. I won't be able to speak to everyone, so I want you to work with a guy I met recently to conduct an organization wide survey. His name is Jack Griffin. I want you to coordinate with his group and have the survey results ready for review in the next two weeks. When I spoke with Jack this morning he told me about a cutting edge survey that can be conducted on line and will compare us against 117 best practices." Bob looked at his notes, "It's called *Virtual CEO*[1] and I think you'll be impressed. Here's the proposal with all the information."

Bob handed him the proposal and then sat back and looked at the ceiling for a moment, and then said, "Doug, this can be the last thing you do here, or the first meaningful thing. Are you willing to at least think about staying?"

Doug thought for a minute, taking the time to finish his drink. "Can I let you know tomorrow, Bob, I want to talk it over with my

---

[1] *Virtual CEO* provides assessments that, among other things, compare organizational and Board performance to industry best practices.

wife before I make a decision. There's quite a bit of money in the new job, and I don't want to stay if things remain the same."

"I don't blame you," said Bob with an understanding look on his face. "Let's get the survey started first thing tomorrow, and let me know your decision. I'm sure we can do something about a raise, especially with your new duties in human development. And by the way Doug, congratulations on the Masters degree, I had no idea you were even going to school. What, did you go nights to get it?"

"Yes. I completed it in eighteen months. It felt really good to finish."

The two wrapped up their meeting and planned to meet the next day. Doug was not happy that Bob had hired a survey company before checking with him, but decided to put that detail aside until he spoke with Jack Griffin.

CONSIDER

- HR has two sides: Development and Compliance. Each area is unique and requires a different skill set to run well. Compliance is about details and risk aversion. Development is about new possibilities, growth and taking a chance.

- When was the last time you conducted an employee survey of any type?

- Which way is your employee turnover trending?

- How many of your best people are looking for new opportunities?

- How many of your people are engaged in higher education?

- Are you encouraging growth as well as compliance?

- If you don't know the answers with certainty, you may be in trouble.

CHAPTER 7

THE CONSULTANT'S SECOND PHONE CALL

There is such a simple elegance to life, a simple set of questions.
Who am I? What am I capable of? Why am I here?

Earlier, when Bob had the idea of conducting an employee survey, he had called Jack to get some advice. Jack told him about a new corporate assessment tool his company used called *Virtual CEO* and had sent over a proposal for Bob to consider.

"Hi, Jack. Good to talk to you again."

"Thanks. How did your first staff meeting go?" asked Jack.

"It was interesting. But before I forget, your *Virtual CEO* assessment proposal looked good so I've asked Doug Martin, our Director of Human Resources to call you and set it up as soon as you can."

"He already called, Bob. He seemed really excited. I have him working with my people. He said you had a sense of urgency so we will be live on-line in two days."

"That's fast. Thanks. I'll be talking with Doug later this morning."

"That's good because I've asked him to help you prepare and send out the announcement to your people so they will be able to get it done in the time-frame you requested."

Bob shifted the conversation. "I don't know how much you know, but prior to the Friday surprise, as it's now being referred to around here, I'd been in Europe for the past year as VP/GM of European Ops. And, I've got to tell you, Jack, a lot has changed while I've been away. I thought I knew the players pretty well before, but in this new role I don't recognize some of them. And now, well, I don't know if they all accept me as the interim CEO. What do you think?"

"When Jesus Christ went home to Nazareth, He was just Joe's Kid. That's who you are right now, Bob, Joe's Kid. They don't see you as the Savior; they see you as the sales and marketing guy who's been out of the loop in Europe the last twelve months," Jack quipped.

"Joe's Kid, that's a good one," Bob laughed.

"The question is, do you have the time to spend convincing them you're the man for the job? In my experience, the number one reason new leaders fail is their inability to re-align and engage their organizations behind a new course of action fast enough. As a high tech CEO you only have about five quarters[2] to make a difference before your job is at risk," Jack said. "And your VPs are, literally, just the tip of the iceberg. Imagine how the rest of the organization is feeling."

"I'm beginning to get the picture," said Bob.

"Conventional wisdom says it takes three to five years to create effective alignment, but, in my experience, it can be done in 90 days. Which one do you want?" asked Jack.

Bob confessed, "I spoke with Phil last night, and he tells me you're serious about the 90 days. Forgive my skepticism, but it's really hard to take seriously. What do you do?"

"I get that a lot," Jack admitted. But I can guarantee you that in 90 days you can have a newly aligned organization with a greatly enhanced ability to attack the mission critical issues you're facing. But that's just the beginning, of course. We can help you get your leadership and management team and the rest of the organization fully engaged, but it takes a real leader to keep them engaged."

"So what's your definition of engaged?" asked Bob.

"Engaged means that everyone in the company, including you, feels challenged, appreciated, personally responsible and part of a game worth playing."

"And you can help me do that? You can create that kind of alignment in 90 days?" asked Bob.

"If that's what you're committed to, yes," said Jack. "But the first step is for us to schedule two days together so you can personally experience what makes 90 days possible. I can come to

---

[2] According to a 2004 study by Burson-Marsteller, today's CEO has only 5 earnings quarters, on average, to prove themselves.

you or you can come to sunny Southern California. Which do you prefer?"

"Two days? Wow, I just don't have two days right now," protested Bob.

"I understand, and that's exactly why you need to do it. You see, you're so used to working 'in' the company putting out fires you just can't see how you can take the time to work 'on' the company. Not unusual. Unfortunately, Jim had the same problem. And that's partly why we never got together. But believe me, Bob, it's critically important. The Board is counting on you to set a new direction and make things better. At the end of our two days you'll know exactly what you are going to do to accomplish what the Board expects. Your life will become a lot easier," Jack promised.

"What are we going to do that takes two days?" asked Bob.

"Well, we're going to address three leadership principles – secrets really – not widely understood or practiced in the contemporary business world. Principles that, when experienced throughout your organization, will exponentially transform your ability to quickly align and grow the company. You do know that Phil only recommended me because he was assured of improved financial results, don't you?"

"That's good to hear. But go on with your leadership principles or secrets, or whatever you call them."

THE THREE LEADERSHIP PRINCIPLES

- To be Powerful in your life, you must first understand and master yourself.
- To be Powerful with others, you must first understand humanity and master relationships.
- To be Powerful in the world, we must learn to co-create and master a game worth playing.

"They're leadership principles, Bob. The secret lies in how to make each happen. So, the first leadership principle is, to be Powerful in your life, especially if you want to lead others, you first have to fully understand and master yourself. This first principle sets the foundation for personal integrity."

Bob thought to himself, "I know perfectly well who I am. What's he talking about?"

"The second principle, Bob, is to be Powerful with others, you must first understand and master what it is to be human. Effective relationships, with your people, customers, strategic partners and the Board depend upon your ability to fully understand and appreciate what drives people and being able to authentically relate to them."

Bob heard himself thinking, "Jack, did you run troops in a war zone? I damn well know how to command people." He actually found himself feeling a little incredulous that Jack would think he didn't know how to build relationships.

"And lastly," continued Jack, "to be Powerful in the world, we must be able to co-create a sustainable game that's worth playing. Briefly, that means you've got to be able to quickly engage every single person in the organization behind what it is you want.

"Remember, Bob, you only have five quarters to prove yourself before the Board begins to question their decision to appoint you CEO."

That got Bob's attention as much as the first time Jack had said it.

"So, to summarize, our first day together will be focused solely on who you are as a leader and what it is you really want for your life. We will unleash what we refer to as *the exponential power of your own unique Purpose & Passion*. In fact you'll actually articulate your Purpose by the end of the day."

"You mean who I am?" questioned Bob. This was sounding way too corny, too woo-woo and too much like a waste of time.

"Yes, Bob, *who you are*," said Jack with an amazing degree of confidence in his voice. Bob continued to be silent but his skepticism radiated over the phone. Jack couldn't help but notice, but continued anyway.

"Our second day is three-fold, Bob. First, you'll develop and articulate a compelling future for the organization that's fully in alignment with who you are as a leader. Second, you will articulate a strategic initiative for the organization, and third, we'll develop a roadmap to bring the organization into alignment with you and your plans."

Bob was more interested in the second day's agenda than the first, and was actually beginning to get more intrigued, but still he said, "Listen, Jack, I'm not entirely sure that I can afford to spend the two days, at least not right now. I have a bunch of things that I need to look into here and I've got to finish the quarter above water. But I'm willing to schedule the time together," he surprised himself by quickly looking through his calendar, "six weeks from now, right after my first official Board meeting. I'll have to get back to you with the exact dates, but I'll come to you. Okay?"

"When you're ready," said Jack. "But I'd like to get together with you and Doug to review the Virtual CEO results in the next two weeks though."

"No problem. I'll be working directly with Doug on that and he'll have my schedule, so if you could coordinate with him that would be great. It will be good to finally meet you," said Bob.

"Likewise," said Jack. "Listen, Bob, if we're not going to get together for six weeks, I have a suggestion if you're interested."

"Yeah, go ahead."

"Spend some part of your time visiting the guys in the field and really listen to them. Not just the managers, Bob, but the engineers, administrators, technicians, and quality people as well," Jack counseled.

"Good advice," said Bob "I'd planned to do that."

"Would you like a few questions you can ask people that will keep their answers specific?" asked Jack.

"Sure," said Bob, as he quickly jotted down Jack's two suggestions.

- What's going well that you feel good about?
- What's not going so well that we can learn from?

"Thanks, Jack. These will be helpful."

"And, Bob," said Jack. "We don't charge by the hour. If you

need someone to bounce some ideas off, feel free to call me anytime."

"Thanks, Jack, and I'll look forward to seeing you soon."

Later that morning Doug popped in and shared the progress he had made with Jack's group. They only had to spend fifteen minutes reviewing the survey announcement to the employees because Doug had already created a draft for Bob to consider.

"Really good work Doug, I really appreciate you taking the ball on this. By the way, did you have a chance to talk our situation over with Diane?"

Bob was glad he had asked Rebecca to bring him Doug's file, so he'd know Doug's wife's name. He had also asked Neil to work out an improved compensation package for Doug so he'd be able to act quickly if Doug showed any willingness to stay.

"Thanks for asking Bob. I did. Just like me, she's open to the idea. What did you have in mind?

"I cleared this with Neil this morning. Beginning today, you'll report directly to me. You will still have to oversee the compliance parts of HR, but I'd like you to expand your duties to include human development as well. I'm very interested in moving out of our Neanderthal phase."

Doug just smiled at the comment.

"And, of course, your new salary will be commensurate with your expanded role."

"Thank you, Bob, but what exactly will the new job entail?"

Like I said yesterday, I'm not really sure. It looks like we'll both be in flux for awhile. But I'm working with Jack Griffin and I'm sure he'll have some suggestions for us. Take advantage of the survey to get to know Jack and his people. We may be working with them a lot in the next year."

Doug was still a little concerned about Jack and his people being thrust on him, but decided to withhold judgment until after he met with them in person.

Off and on for the next six weeks Bob was on airplanes visiting the troops in the field and in each regional office. He took groups of field personnel to dinner and dug into the good, the bad and the ugly. People opened up to Bob's questions in a constructive manner. His digging pissed off a few of his VPs but delighted the line managers and staff. He began to see the roots of the tension between his senior staff as simple misunderstandings, and he saw that the morale in the trenches was awful, just as Neil and Doug Martin had predicted. Some of their key people were indeed looking for jobs.

In between trips he found himself getting involved in putting out fires between departments and having to visit clients to smooth their feathers. In one case he made the mistake of promising a client fixes that only ended up causing more problems for the troops back at the ranch. But they got through the quarter with a few bluebirds, and that, he thought, would buy him some time with the Board. He would be wrong about that.

During his time on the road, Bob took Jack up on his offer to be a sounding board. Bob blind-copied Jack on some e-mails that were flying back and forth between departments which were beginning to give shape to the true state of affairs within the company. There was a lot of covering ass and finger pointing going on with precious little problem resolution. The results of the *Virtual CEO* survey pointed to not only mission critical issues, but to how little was being done to resolve them because of the lack of internal focus and teamwork. Jack and Bob agreed to move their meeting up if they could. Bob was beginning to see the wisdom of pulling what Jack called a *hard reset* on the company because, at this rate, the necessary changes he had in mind would take more time than he had.

THE FIRST BOARD MEETING

The Board meeting in San Francisco was very uncomfortable for Bob. "Were they always this challenging to Jim?" he wondered. While Bob had been acting CEO for less than 60 days, the Board clearly expected miracles. Frankly, he wished he could have delivered more positive news.

"Bob," said Phil Knight, standing in the doorway to the small conference room where Bob had camped out. "That was pretty rough in there. Can we talk for a few minutes?"

"Sure, why not," said Bob, a little resigned.

Phil walked in and shut the door behind him. He sat down and looked closely at Bob.

"Was there a reason you were so defensive that I should know about?"

Bob looked up at Phil. Then stood, turned and looked out the window. "I don't know, Phil. I felt like I was being attacked. Maybe I was just tired from all the travel. I don't know. I didn't want to give them a bunch of excuses, so I didn't exactly know what to tell them."

"We're only trying to get a truthful read on what's happening, just like you. The Board is tired of not knowing what's going on, Bob. In the past, Jim always felt he had to have *the* answer and rarely asked us for advice. Hell, Bob, that's what we're here for. Don't be afraid to let us know what's happening. Three of us have been CEOs, so we understand pretty well what it's like to be in your shoes. And after the Enron and Arthur Anderson fiascos, and especially after having to spend over a million bucks this quarter to be in compliance with Sarbanes-Oxley[3], no one on the Board is going to be kept in the dark, even if they have to go visit your people in the field themselves."

They were both silent. Bob didn't know what to say and felt the best thing to do was listen. Phil seemed supportive and he would need his support in the future.

Phil continued, "You have to get the Board on your side, Bob, and the best way to do that is to engage them. I understand your reluctance, but as I understand Jim already shared with you, Jim didn't leave solely because of his marriage. The Board was putting a lot of pressure on him because of his lone ranger attitude."

---

[3] The Sarbanes-Oxley Act, signed into law on 30 July 2002 by President George W. Bush, is considered the most significant change to federal securities laws in the United States since the New Deal. It came in the wake of a series of corporate financial scandals, including those affecting Enron, Arthur Andersen, and WorldCom.

"So what do you suggest?" Bob countered still somewhat defensively.

"Have you spoken to Jack Griffin yet?" Phil queried.

"Yes. He's quite a character. I must admit, he pissed me off when I first spoke with him, but over the past month he's become a good sounding board. I've been sharing our situation with him and he's been a good listener. We agreed that I needed to spend some time in the field before he and I got together for his two day coaching session," said Bob, stretching the truth a little, "but we had our first face-to-face a few weeks ago. His group conducted an organizational assessment of the entire company, from top to bottom. I thought the results were pretty ugly. But Jack just smiled and said it was just a temporary situation."

"That's Jack. And when are you going to do the two-day with him?" Phil prodded.

"We're going to talk later today and I'll try to set it up for this Friday and Saturday." Bob acquiesced.

"Good. So tell me, what have you found out in your travels?" Phil wanted to know.

Relaxing a little, Bob said "Well, my senior staff is spending more time than ever putting out fires of their own making and, while everyone is talking, no one is hearing what the other is saying. Frankly, it's pretty brutal. Morale is in the toilet and development throughput is at a standstill because most of Engineering is tied up fixing bugs from the last release, which puts customer growth on the back burner and further cuts licensing revenue. Put the lack of sales into the mix and it's pretty grim." Bob admitted.

"Is that all?" laughed Phil.

"Actually, it's not. I installed an escalation process that I thought would help give us an early warning to things going south, but it just ended up pissing everyone off. The word in the company is that I don't trust anyone, which is true in a way."

Phil just laughed again. "The best laid plans of mice and men. Listen, Bob, had you shared exactly that with the Board this morning it would have been a much easier meeting. The truth stated simply goes a long way. You might want to give the Board members a call off-line. And, let me know how it goes with Jack. Call me on Sunday."

"Thanks, Phil. I will," Bob promised, referring to his call on Sunday, but remaining uncommitted to calling the other Board members for now.

As soon as Phil left, Bob decided to call Jack Griffin to finalize their get-together. Fortunately, Bob had been able to report to Phil that he and Jack had been talking, but it was clearly time to get together. He noticed his former reluctance to meet with Jack had all but disappeared. He pulled up Jack's number on his cell phone and hit "send".

"Hi Jack. Listen, I've been in San Francisco this week meeting with the Board. It's been a challenging experience. I can get down to you on Thursday evening. I know its short notice, but can we do our two day thing on Friday and Saturday?"

"No problem," said Jack. "I'll have to shift a few things, but I'm looking forward to getting together with you. Give me your flight information, and I'll pick you up when you get in."

"Great. I'd appreciate that."

"Well," Bob thought after his call to Jack, "I'm committed now. But how the heck can I spend an entire day talking about myself?"

CONSIDER

- How many of your people do you treat like "Joe's Kid?"

- The biggest reason for CEO, executive and manager failure is their inability to engage their people quickly.

- If you could shift the culture of your organization within 90 days, what would you shift it to?

- Are you too busy working 'in' your organization to work 'on' it?

- Can you say with certainty that you understand and have mastered yourself?

- Can you say with certainty that you understand and appreciate what it is to be human and have mastered the art of relationships?

- Can you say with certainty that you have co-created a game worth playing – for yourself and others?

- What's going well you can feel good about?

- What's not going so well you can learn from?

- On a scale of 1-10, how well do you really know the people you work with?

- Sarbanes-Oxley says, in effect, CEOs can't be trusted. What does that mean to you in terms of your reputation?

- How many of your policies say "We don't trust you?"

- The truth stated simply goes a long way. How often do you feel compelled to obfuscate the truth?

CHAPTER 8

VISIONING DAY ONE

"Your vision will become clear only when you look into your heart.
Who looks outside, dreams. Who looks inside, awakens."
– Carl Jung

Jack picked Bob up at Burbank Airport – now called Bob Hope Field – and got him to the hotel in Westlake Village at 8:00 PM. They had a quiet dinner in the hotel and made plans to meet at Jack's office a few blocks away at 8:00 AM.

In the morning, Bob decided to walk to Jack's office located in "The WaterCourt." This office complex in Westlake Village was surrounded by park-like grounds containing waterfalls, streams and ponds, which created a serene and calming ambiance. As he stood at the railing outside of Jack's office door, Bob looked down at the pond and noticed eight bright yellow ducklings swimming in a row behind their mother. The mother duck stopped cold and the eight ducklings scattered all over the place. He thought to himself, "*Momentum counts* – so I'd better keep moving."

He turned around, opened the door and entered Jack's office. The smell of fresh brewed coffee was in the air. "God I love the smell of napalm in the morning!" he thought, laughing out loud with a smile on his face.

"Good morning, you must be Mr. Harris. I'm Beverly, Jack's assistant."

"Yes, I am. Nice to meet you, Beverly."

"Thank you. We're all set for you, so may I show you to the Visioning Room?"

"Hmmm, a Visioning Room," thought Bob. "What are they going to do, hook me up to some kind of virtual reality machine?"

Along the way, Beverly introduced Bob to some of the other partners of the firm. He'd heard from Phil that each of them had been former CEOs themselves.

"Are all the partners former CEOs?" he asked Beverly.

"Yes. We think it makes sense that our consultants have a perspective that's similar to our clients when they deliver our message"

"And what's the message?" Bob asked.

"First, for leaders to succeed, *they must know themselves fully,*" she said, putting sequential fingers up with each statement, "second, *they must understand and appreciate what it is to be human – be a master of relationships,* and third, *they must be able to co-create a game worth playing,*" said Beverly. "All true leadership begins with that foundation, Mr. Harris. Without it you can manage, but can't lead, at least not in a reactive world. Our work gives CEOs a conscious choice between their Ego and Purpose, and with it, tremendous freedom."

"Whoa," thought Bob. He was impressed that Jack's assistant was so clear and concise. But he still wasn't sure what it could mean for him.

When they got to the Visioning Room, Beverly motioned Bob to have a seat, poured him a cup of freshly brewed coffee, and served the condiments with a tray of pastries, fruit and yogurt.

"Help yourself to some breakfast, Mr. Harris. Jack will be right in." Beverly put the tray down in front of Bob, closed the French doors and disappeared down the hall.

The room was all white with offset lighting. There was the soothing sound of a fountain and soft music playing in the background. He noticed green plants in the corner and a large oil painting on the far wall. The painting's perspective was from the bedroom balcony of a hacienda looking out over a Spanish mission along the coastline of an ocean.

"Very pleasing," he thought.

In the center of the room was a puzzle of glass tables fitted together into one, surrounded by three comfortable chairs. A flip chart easel stood in one corner.

On the wall directly across from where he was sitting were two pieces of chart paper stuck to the wall side by side. There was a black line drawn horizontally, roughly in the middle, from the left side of the first paper to the far side of the other. On the upper right hand side of the paper was a bright yellow star.

"Good morning Bob," said Jack as he walked quietly into the room, and shook Bob's hand. "It's good to finally have you here. Are you ready for an amazing day?"

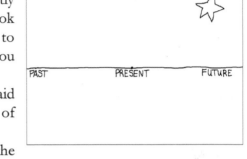

"I guess we'll see," said Bob, still with some degree of skepticism.

The two had spent the previous evening in general conversation becoming more at ease with each other, so this morning, Jack got right to the point.

"To begin our time together I'd like to start by 'Clearing.' Are you familiar with the practice, Bob?"

"No, what do you mean?"

"Well, we often come into meetings thinking about something else – the meeting we just left, a disagreement with a staff member or some other unfinished business or upset. We're halfway through the current meeting before we're able to clear our minds enough to give the topic at hand our full attention. Have you ever had that experience?"

"I guess we all have," said Bob.

"Everything we discuss over the next two days is confidential and will not leave this room, so," said Jack, "to start the clearing process, what's on your mind?"

Bob thought about it for a minute.

"Well, I'm in the middle of figuring out how to react to my Board. It was a rocky meeting the other day, and I guess I feel like I'm not living up to their expectations. They have three big concerns that Jim was – according to them – not able to get under control. The first is to *finish the PDQ integration*. After almost a year, it still seems to be a mess. The second is to *get our leadership leading instead of fighting*. And the third is to *dramatically reduce expenses, improve throughput and increase revenue*."

"Is that all?" smiled Jack.

"Unfortunately, no, it's not. Our time to market for new products has taken a nosedive. Although, in fairness to the PDQ guys, we were slipping on that before they came aboard. And our low morale, it turns out, hasn't been lost on the Board. Two of the Board members made visits to the field and as you might expect, have developed a critical view of how we are managing the integration, which, as I said, has been going on for over a year. So, as you might expect, my first official Board meeting was a catalyst for me to be here."

"Good. So if we address the Board's concerns, along with your own, of course, that would be a good thing?"

"Yes, I'd say so."

INTENTIONS

Jack wrote the three expectations articulated by the Board on the flip chart under the headline 'Intentions'. The word 'expectation' was, in Jack's mind far too passive for what they had to accomplish.

"Since you seem to be adopting the Board's desires as your own, what additional personal intentions do you have for our two days together?"

"Well, learn more about myself and my leadership style. Maybe learn to be an effective CEO faster than I would on my own. Tie what I learn here into results for the organization. And maybe discover some useful things about my people I'm not seeing yet."

Jack listed Bob's intentions below the two defined by the Board.

"Good. Everything on the list is fair game for our

Intentions

1. Integrate PDQ quickly into the rest of the company
2. Get our leadership leading instead of fighting
3. Reduce expenses and improve throughput and sales revenue
4. Learn more about myself and my leadership style
5. Learn to be an effective CEO faster than I would on my own
6. Quickly tie what I learn here into results for the organization
7. Discover some useful things about my people I'm not seeing yet

conversation," Jack summarized, "but obviously, we will not accomplish numbers 1, 2 or 3 over the next two days. Those will take a few month's effort on the part of the entire organization.

"I understand," said Bob, "but I want to discuss how to accomplish them!"

"Of course," said Jack

Jack paused for a moment and poured a cup of coffee, and then sat across from Bob so he could look him in the eyes. Bob sat back in his chair.

"I've adopted two important rules for working with people from a mentor of mine that I'd like to use with you. Do you mind if I share them with you?" asked Jack.

"No, I don't."

"The first rule is – don't believe a word I say!"

"Pardon me?" Bob asked with a quizzical look on his face.

"*Don't believe a word I say!*" said Jack with a small laugh. "You see, Bob, I can only come from my own experience, and what I say may be right for me but not for you. Our job here is to identify your own experience and voice. So as we go forward, try on what I have to say over the next two days and if it fits, keep it. If not, well…"

"Dump it?" offered Bob.

"Exactly, or, at least, set it aside for future consideration."

"And the second rule?" Bob asked.

"The second rule is to participate in these next two days 100%."

"Okay. I accept your rules." Bob agreed.

"So," Jack continued, "during our time together, I may have some observations about you that I'd like to share. If something does come up, are you open to me providing you with feedback or coaching?"

"Fine with me," said Bob as he privately wondered what Jack would observe and what the feedback would be.

"Excellent," said Jack.

"Is there anything you'd like to know about us before we get started?" Jack asked.

"I admired Beverly's ability to describe what you do, but why don't you tell me more about your firm. I'm here mostly because Phil so highly recommended you, but I can't say I know much about you."

"Fair enough," said Jack.

"Our Mission is Creating Extraordinary Organizations," explained Jack as he wrote on a flip chart, "by unleashing the exponential power of Purpose & Passion that's virtually untapped in today's organizations.

> Creating Extraordinary
> Organizations
> by Unleashing the Exponential
> Power of Purpose & Passion

"Identifying your Purpose & Passion will transform your world view and what it means to be a CEO. You will shift your role from being a 'Chief Executive Officer' expected to know it all, to being a leader committed to Creating an Extraordinary Organization. This is virgin territory, Bob, because there is no 'one way' to do that. You will enter into an on-going inquiry, if you will."

"Mmmm," said Bob, as he kept his face expressionless. He was open to hearing more, but he wasn't sure if this was hype or real.

> **Leadership Secrets**
>
> 1. To be Powerful in your life, you must first understand and master yourself
>
> 2. To be Powerful with others, you must first understand humanity and master relationships
>
> 3. To be Powerful in the world, we must learn to co-create and master a game worth playing

"Remember in one of our recent phone conversations you asked me about the 'secrets' of being a successful CEO? We will be exploring them in depth throughout these two days."

"We're beginning today with principle number one: *To be powerful in your life, you must first understand and master yourself.* This is the first step to a higher level of awareness. In the first part of this inquiry you'll answer three important questions," Jack continued as he wrote on the chart page, "Who am I? What am I capable of? Why am I here?

"Ultimately, your answers to these questions will lead you to the unique meaning of your life – to what we define as self-knowledge."

"I noticed that you switch between leadership secrets and principles," said Bob, "what's the difference?"

> **Three Questions**
>
> 1. Who am I?
> 2. What am I capable of?
> 3. Why am I here?

"Good question," said Jack. "To be clear, these are the three key principles of leadership. The *secret* is how to affect them in your life and in your company."

Jack paused for a moment before he asked Bob, "I imagine you've read a fair amount of leadership literature, haven't you?"

"Not as much as you might expect, but yes," acknowledged Bob, "I've read a fair amount over the years."

"Well then, perhaps you've noticed there is precious little mentioned about *how* you get to know yourself?"

"I don't recall much," returned Bob.

"That's because the world assumes you'll magically come to self-knowledge all by yourself with practice and self-discipline. And indeed some of us do, usually after some life changing experience that has us deeply question our lives. Divorces, losing a loved one, losing a job, a near death experience, sickness and going broke are some typical examples. We are then faced with a choice. We can either find something positive in the experience and move on in our lives with a higher level of confidence, or we can feel lost and remain stuck. Unfortunately, many don't recognize the choice and by default, remain stuck.

"Fortunately, we've found a way to get you to self-knowledge in a single day, without a lot of the drama or trauma."

"That's a big claim Jack – that you can actually get me to self-knowledge that quickly."

"It is, isn't it?" Jack said smiling. "And yes, we can actually do this – in fact, we'll do it today. You see, Bob, most books about leadership and self development suggest that to be successful we should strive to be just like somebody else. Steven Covey's *The Seven Habits of Highly Successful People* and Jim Collins' *Good to Great* come to mind. These are amazingly good books, classics that go to great lengths to describe powerfully effective men and women who were successful in another time. And then they go on to suggest that for you and me to be as successful we need to model the behavior of the individuals described in their books. This is a common message to people in every walk of life. To be better, to have more, to get rich, to lose weight – to be a leader – we should do what others have done. Not a bad strategy actually, but how many of us actually follow through?"

Jack continued with his explanation, "There is a name for this approach, Bob, but it's not called leadership, its called modeling. Modeling can be a very effective strategy. However, to integrate these habits fully, these learned behaviors must align intrinsically with *who we really are*, with our beliefs, and with our own unique set of values, or they're not sustainable. If not aligned, the ideals, values and behaviors of others rarely make it to 'habit' status within us. This is why we so strongly emphasize the importance of really, authentically, knowing yourself before attempting any behavioral changes."

Jack shifted in his seat and leaned toward Bob.

"Every person actually has the ability to be an effective leader at some level. However, most people, including CEOs, have not been provided with the tools to help them access their own inner resources. And it's using these inner resources that make a leader great."

"So you are saying leaders are born, not made?" challenged Bob.

"I'm saying that leaders are born and need to be developed," Jack replied. "One of the most important premises in our work is that *everyone has leadership potential including the basics they need to lead within them already*. Our job is to first help clients recognize this to be true, and second, help them articulate what that means to them and then, third, coach them to mastery in that area."

"Okay" said Bob, "I have another question. How exactly do you define *inner resources*? What are the elements you're talking about?"

"There are three intrinsic elements: *your Values, Purpose and Passion*. When you become clear about these three elements, which comprise the foundation of character, then and only then can you authentically choose how you will *be*. Until then, most of us simply react to the circumstances around us.

"You obviously have been on the fast track in developing much of your own potential throughout your entire life. You may or may not have had the good fortune to have been coached by masters. Regardless, I believe it's time for you, as CEO, to become a master yourself."

Jack let that sit for a few seconds.

"What do you mean, 'become a master?'" asked Bob?

"When you finally articulate who you are, Bob, you will be faced with the biggest challenge of your life – *being who you were meant to be in the world*. The outer world and a good part of your inner self will do everything in its power to dissuade you from expressing who you really are. In fact the biggest impediment to you being you will be your own Ego self. So self-mastery, the mastery over your own Ego, is critical to your self fulfillment."

While Jack was talking, Bob became aware that he was upset. "What am I doing here?" he heard himself thinking. Then Bob noticed a familiar feeling – tightness around his heart. He wanted to tell Jack he knew exactly who the hell he was already, that he was already successful, and …

"Bob, you may experience a wide range of feelings throughout the day," interjected Jack, as though he knew what Bob was thinking, "Did you see *The Karate Kid*?"

"Sure," this was spooky, thought Bob.

"Remember the 'wax on, wax off' sequence?"

"Sort of."

"Well, in that scene Mr. Miyagi, the Master, has Daniel, the Karate Kid, waxing Miyagi's cars. Mr. Miyagi was very particular in how Daniel was to accomplish the task. Daniel was to apply the wax with his left hand in a counter-clock-wise direction, and wipe it off with his right hand in a clockwise direction. This was all well and good for the first car, but when Daniel came to the master and said he was finished, the master told him to do the other three cars as well. Daniel was not happy, and began thinking the worst, that Miyagi wasn't a Master at all, and was just taking advantage of him. When he finally finished all the cars, Daniel challenged Mr. Miyagi's intentions and he quickly learned the truth. What was the truth, Bob, do you remember now?"

"That what Miyagi was telling Daniel to do – wax on, wax off – would make sense later, and it did. Miyagi was teaching Daniel the basics of defense," said Bob making Karate movements and gaining back some of his equilibrium.

"Good, keep that in mind all day, will you?"

Bob smiled and said, "Sure."

"Great. Now, I want you to consider this line I've drawn across this paper," said Jack pointing to the two sheets of chart paper taped together on the wall with the line drawn across the middle

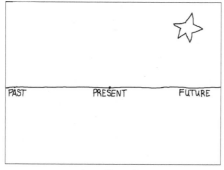

and a bright yellow star in the upper right hand corner.

"I want you to make believe that this line is your personal time line," said Jack. "It has a past, present and future, and I want you to imagine that it goes off on both sides to infinity. What you see on the flip chart represents just your life on earth. Are you with me?"

"Sure," said Bob, mentally trying to stay in neutral and resisting the urge to roll his eyes.

"Good. Because you're so cooperative I'm going to give you a 100 year run."

Bob laughed, "As long as you don't charge me extra," he said.

CONSIDER

- Momentum creates a draft that pulls people along. In whatever you do, create momentum.

- Clearing at the beginning and ending of a meeting can give you a clear picture of where to begin and how to follow up with participants.

- Intention is the first element of creation.

- The exponential power of individual and organizational Purpose and Passion are virtually untapped in the majority of today's companies.

- As Chief Executive Officer, you are expected to know it all. As a leader committed to Creating Extraordinary Organizations, you are open to it all.

- Can you articulate who you are?

- Can you articulate what you are capable of?

- Can you articulate why you are here?

- Modeling others is effective, especially when you are intrinsically aligned with their behavior.

- Everyone has leadership potential and the basics they need to lead within them already. Your job as leader is to help yourself and others gain access to it.

- There are three intrinsic elements to your Character: Values, Purpose and Passion.

- The biggest challenge in life is being who you were meant to be. The outer world, and a good part of your inner self, will do everything in its power to dissuade you from expressing who you really are.

- Self mastery, the mastery over your own Ego, is critical to your self fulfillment.

CHAPTER 9

APPRECIATING THE PAST

"It is what we think we already know that often prevents us from learning."
— Claude Bernard

Jack sat back in his chair, looked Bob in the eye and asked, "So Bob, what was your very first thought or memory?"

"What was my what?" said Bob.

"What was your very first thought or memory?" Jack repeated.

Jack just sat there with an expectant look on his face, and Bob started to think to himself, "What the hell kind of question is that?" Bob asked a bit more sharply than he intended, "Is this going to be some kind of counseling session where we review my childhood and my parents' treatment of me so we can figure out why I behave like I do?"

Jack was used to this kind of defensiveness, so he answered calmly, "I realize that this may be a new and different situation for you to be in. It's intended to be that way, precisely so that you can begin to see yourself in new ways. The process does require your trust and willingness to participate, even if you think there are parts that are ridiculous, pointless, or even painful. Do you remember just a few minutes ago, I said one rule was that you participate 100%? You willingly agreed when you didn't know what to expect. Now that you have a small taste, I am asking again if you are willing to fully participate – despite your discomfort. Without this willingness, there's no point in continuing. This is your time and your experience and I will genuinely respect your decision."

Bob had to simply sit and stew for a few moments. Jack knew this and said, "I'll bring some fresh coffee and water and give you a chance to decide what you'd like to do."

While Jack was gone, Bob closed his eyes and took a few deep breaths. "Damn, this was even harder than the Board meeting. All of this talk about being *who you were meant to be* and *Ego-self* was unnerving. What to do? Stay or go? Go back or move forward?

Bob opened his eyes and looked at the blank chart. "Oh, what the hell," he thought, "I'm here, so I might as well go through with this." And then it came to him.

Just as Jack walked back into the room, Bob muttered "I was in my playpen." The memory and his words surprised him. They just popped out of his mouth like they had a mind of their own. Like somehow the little kid in the crib was making it known that the experience indeed had happened.

"Good. Now, in your mind's eye," said Jack, not missing a beat as he put down the coffee and water, "take a look around and notice. Is anyone there with you? What's happening around you?" Jack queried.

Bob closed his eyes, sat back and heard himself say, "My mother is there, and my two sisters. We are out next to the pool. It's sunny. My sisters and her friends are swimming in the pool. We're at the house in Texas and it's hot."

"How old are you?" asked Jack

"Two," said Bob. He was surprised again at how certain he was.

"And then what happened?"

For the rest of the morning Bob looked at his life in a way that he never had before. He looked at his early childhood, his friends, his siblings, the environment, how the family got along, the highlights and defining moments in grade school, high school, college, grad school, the military and his career. He talked about his triumphs and failures, his relationships and his jobs. He talked about how he felt and what he wanted and where he saw he was today. Jack listened to Bob in a way he had never been listened to before. The guy he initially didn't like, who he thought was a kook, drew him out like only a trusted friend could. Bob watched as Jack captured the highlights of his life up on the time line on the wall.

As Bob looked at his life's events he was amazed. In the beginning, Bob thought he'd just throw out a few significant highlights, but as he talked, he felt good about revealing more and more aspects of his life. He found that he enjoyed recalling both the good and the bad times and that from this perspective and in this moment, it didn't look all that bad. He never thought he would have so much to say. But here he was looking at the sheets on the wall covered with his life. Everything was up there, even though some of it was left unsaid and buried between the lines, all the way up to the recent Board meeting in San Francisco.

Bob began to see that there were more than a few choices he made during his life that could have gone differently.

"So," said Jack, "let's look at this rich and full life. I want you to look it over very carefully and tell me, what themes and patterns you notice, and then record them on the flip chart."

After looking at his timeline for a few minutes Bob wrote his observations on the chart paper.

"Good work," said Jack. "What else do you notice about your life?"

"What do you mean?" Bob puzzled.

"Well, look at all that has happened. How much of it was planned? How much of it was a reaction to circumstance?"

"I don't understand," said Bob.

"We live in a reactive world, Bob. If I were to draw a chart of how your life has gone so far, it would look sort of like this, wouldn't it?" Jack led Bob's gaze with his drawing.

"Sure," said Bob "seems reasonable."

"So, Bob, as you look at this graph, what does it remind you of?"

"The stock market," he said.

"Good observation. So which of these is true?" asked Jack as he continued to write

> **Themes and Patterns**
>
> - Like leading teams of people
> - Make it a point to know the rules of the game
> - Desire to be challenged
> - Understand the big picture
> - Knowing I can do anything I set my mind to
> - I have the power to spread energy
> - Slow to trust people

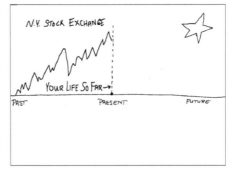

on a new piece of chart paper.

Does the economy affect companies and then the companies affect people? Or, do people affect the companies and then the companies affect the economy?"

"I guess a little of both. It's no secret our business is down because our customers are affected by the economy," Bob answered.

"Your answer is reflective of conventional wisdom," said Jack. "However there's another way to look at this question. In my experience it's who we are being – *our outlooks and our belief systems as CEOs* – that affect our companies, which, in turn, affect the economy."

Economy>Company>People?
Or
People>Company>Economy?

"Interesting," said Bob, "I've heard people refer to self-fulfilling prophecies, but I never related it to my own life. In fact, I never gave it much thought before just now."

"This is just another noticing, Bob, another step toward a higher level of awareness."

"Awareness?" asked Bob.

Jack smiled, then looked down a bit sheepishly and began to tell a story.

"When I was in the Navy I became fond of a certain four-letter word. One day, I was engaged in particularly spirited conversation about the life of a sailor with one of my mates. I hadn't noticed that the Captain was standing on the Bridge wing just a few feet above us. Anyway, after a rather lusty paragraph or two the Captain leaned over the railing and said, "Excuse me, sailor. But do you get a quarter every time you say that word?" While his words were measured, when I turned and looked him in the face, he wasn't sporting what I would call an approving look. He then simply turned and walked back into the bridge, shaking his head as he went."

Bob laughed. "So how does that demonstrate noticing?"

"Well, every time I said the word after that I noticed it. And I also remembered the Captain's comments and his disapproving look. Soon I began to hear the word as it came out of my mouth, then as it began to come out of my mouth, and then when it was just a thought. Finally – and this didn't take long, maybe a day or so – I began to choose whether to say it or not. Finally, I just stopped using the word altogether."

"And?" queried Bob.

"Sometimes we just need to have something called to our attention, to notice – to be *aware* is probably a better word – what we're saying, thinking or doing to be able to stop it. Until then, we are simply unaware, unconscious – *reactive*."

"Funny story," laughed Bob

"Believe me, it wasn't at the time," admitted Jack.

"We have the ability to see more than we can see now. As CEOs we have tremendous impact on the lives of others. There is just no power in believing you are at the effect of life. That's the way the majority of the world thinks, and why so many people see themselves as victims. All the power is in taking personal responsibility, Bob, and in being 'cause' of your world. So our job today is to give you the ability to move from being reactive and at the *effect* of circumstance, to being creative and the *cause* of what happens. Would that be useful?"

"Sure, I guess so," said Bob.

"One of my partners came up with this visual to demonstrate what we are trying to accomplish here," said Jack as he wrote the word REACTION on the chart. Our ability to *see clearly* is buried in the middle of all the reaction," Jack explained, underlining the letter 'C' in the middle of the word reaction.

> To move from
>
> REA**C**TION
> to
> **C**REATION
>
> Move your ability
> to **see** up front!

"And as you move your ability to *see* up front, you automatically gain access to being more creative."

"Well, I still think the world around us forces us to react to our circumstances. Our past dictates our future and I don't see that changing any time soon. Do you?" Bob opined.

"No, I don't think we are forced to react and no, I don't think the past must dictate our future," replied Jack. "And, I predict that your life will change dramatically by the end of today."

Bob didn't yet see what all this wordplay had to do with running the company, or how his life was going to change in any significant way. However, he had somehow crossed a line when he shared his life history and he was committed to seeing what might happen during the remainder of the day. He would wait and see. So far, the day was certainly like nothing else he had ever experienced. And he had to admit, with a smile, that like the Karate Kid, he had a lot of waxing on and waxing off going on in his head.

CONSIDER

- What is your first memory?
- Sequentially reflecting on your life will reveal its themes.
- Wisdom only comes from the past considered.
- To move from Reaction to Creation, move your ability to see up front and get above the chaos.

CHAPTER 10

CORE VALUES & LEARNED ATTRIBUTES

Until called forth, defined and agreed upon, values remain a myth.
Have you ever seen a list of Family Values?

After a break Jack wrote *"Core Values and Learned Attributes"* at the top of the chart and asked Bob, "If you were to think of all the various situations you find yourself in, with your family, on the job, socially and in fun and serious situations, which of your characteristics or traits tend to be consistent across the board?"

Bob quickly posted four words up on the board: Competitive, reliable, curious and relentless. After looking at the page for a while, Bob said that was about it. But Jack proceeded to make room for five more.

"Let's at least fill up the page. I know you're more complex than just these four attributes." Jack explained that there were typically three kinds of words that would make it to the page:

> **Core Values &**
> **Learned Attributes**
>
> - Competitive
> - Reliable
> - Curious
> - Relentless

1. Core Values
2. Supportive Learned Attributes
3. Non-supportive Learned Attributes

"For this conversation, let's assume that Core Values[4] are those attributes you were born with," Jack began. "Learned Attributes are either supportive or non-supportive and, as the name implies, were learned because of some teaching, experience or observation during your lifetime. They were adopted, usually as a result of parental, social or environmental influences, or, as is often

---

[4] The Values process is adapted from the early work of NLP Master David Gordon, one of the original developers of NLP.

the case, traumatic experiences, typically at a very early age."

They continued the exercise and after a few minutes Bob was surprised at how many words he had put up on the board.

After a pause, Bob said, "I think I'm done, Jack. What do we do now?"

Jack said, "We are going to define what each of these words means to you. So, what does it mean to you to be competitive?"

Bob thought for a moment, and then replied.

**Core Values &
Learned Attributes**

- Competitive
- Relentless
- Natural Leader
- Responsible
- Action oriented
- Trustworthy
- Spontaneous

"Well, driven to play the game to win, to give my all toward winning." He noticed his definition wasn't according to Webster, but it was meaningful to him.

"Excellent," said Jack. "Are you complete with that definition?"

"Yes," said Bob.

"So then," continued Jack, "what does it mean to you to be relentless?"

"Never giving up," said Bob.

The two continued until Bob had completed the definition for each word. When they were finished Jack went back yet again to the beginning and asked, "*Have you always been competitive?*"

**Core Values &
Learned Attributes**

- Loving
- Cautious & not trusting
- Energizing
- Caring
- Risk Taker
- Loyal

"I don't know. Mostly, I suppose," Bob admitted.

"*Was there ever a time when you weren't competitive?*" Jack continued.

"Yes, sure, I mean there are times when it's just plain silly to be competitive. Like with my children or my wife for example," Bob answered.

"And how do you feel when you are not competitive with them?" asked Jack.

"No big deal, I don't even think about it," Bob shrugged.

"So what we have just learned is that, in your case, 'competitive' is a learned behavior. It's a behavior that continues to support you because we live in a very competitive world. Had it been a core value, you would not have been able to stand it when you were not competitive, you would have felt you let yourself down," Jack explained.

They went through the rest of the words and found that many were indeed core to him. When he failed to be caring, for example, it caused Bob real pain and regret.

"So tell me about this one," said Jack, pointing to "cautious and not trusting."

"I don't know, I guess I've always been cautious, especially with respect to new people in my life. Like the definition says: Not trusting of others until they prove themselves," Bob determined.

"And have you always been cautious and not trusting?"

"I think so, yes."

"Well, Bob, one thing I know for sure, you were not born with that particular attribute. So, if you will work with me for a while here, I'd like to label this one a non-supportive learned attribute and I'll come back and explain why later – is that okay with you?"

"Okay, sure."

Jack then asked Bob to rate each core value and learned attribute on a scale of 1-10 with 10 being very strong in him and a 1 being present but weak in him. Jack explained that Bob could have as many 10's or 5's or whatever he wanted. When Bob was done he

---

Bob's Core Values

10 <u>Natural Leader</u> - Wanting the best for people. Helping others reach their highest potential. Taking charge when there's a vacuum

10 <u>Responsible</u> - Taking responsibility for the outcome

10 <u>Relentless</u> - Never giving up

10 <u>Spontaneous</u> - Acting on my own to get things done. Action oriented. Rather do something than wait to get it perfect

10 <u>Trustworthy</u> - My word can be counted on. Honesty

9 <u>Energizing</u> - To transfer energy to others

8 <u>Caring</u> - care deeply about the people who are close to me or who are in my charge

8 <u>Risk Taker</u> - Love challenge, experiencing danger, willing to risk my neck when necessary.

7 <u>Loving</u> - Caring about people and loving yourself too

was looking at a finished list complete with his Values, his definitions, and a rating of how strong each was within him.

"When you get into a stressful situation, your tens will kick in before your nines," explained Jack. "And if you have a learned attribute that's strong, it could override a value. For example, 'cautious and not trusting' could override the 'risk taker' in you. Does that make sense?"

"It does," said Bob.

"Good." said Jack, "You will know this because you will feel 'off.' Values don't become real for individuals or groups until they're identified and consciously chosen," Jack added, "For most people, values don't really exist until they are articulated. And you can't assume they exist in people or organizations until then."

"I never thought about my values in this way before," shared Bob. "I'm amazed because as I look at them now, I know they're all an important part of me."

"That's another valuable noticing, Bob. Whether or not we were born with core values or learned them while we were growing up, they are an integral part of us. And when our core values are violated, either by ourselves or someone else, it causes pain – or at the very least, stress.

"Everyone has their own unique set of values, but unfortunately, we aren't always aware of them. And when in reactive mode, we don't always stop to think about how our words or actions might impinge on the core values of others or even violate our own set of values," said Jack.

"So those are my core values?" said Bob, "And these are my supportive learned behaviors?" pointing to the learned behavior sheets. "And what about this one you

---

Supportive Learned Behaviors

10 <u>Competitive</u> - Driven to play the game to win, to give my all toward winning

9 <u>Loyal</u> - Sticking with someone even when they do something stupid

---

Non-Supportive Learned Behavior

10 <u>Cautious and Not Trusting</u> - I am not trusting of others until they prove themselves

marked a non-supportive learned behavior?" How do you know it's non-supportive?"

"We believe that anything that causes us to feel diminished, threatened or gets in the way of our full self expression is a non-supportive behavior that stems from a limiting belief. We will talk more about limiting beliefs tomorrow, especially in how they affect organizations. But for now let me give you an example. A universal limiting belief is, 'I'm not good enough.' Have you ever experienced that one?"

"Who hasn't?" Bob parried.

"Here's a model we call BEAR. Again, we will talk more about it tomorrow, but see if this makes any sense. Our Beliefs guide our Emotions, which inform our Actions, which give us our Results."

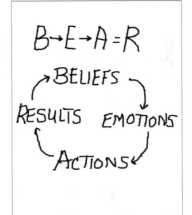

- **Belief** - Not good enough
- **Emotion** -Fearful
- **Action**- Slow/cautious
- **Result**- Less than ideal

"Looks like a self fulfilling prophecy," said Bob.

"Exactly, and it gets worse. Because limiting beliefs are invisible until called into question, we don't even acknowledge them as an issue, yet they may be the biggest issue in our lives."

"What do you mean the biggest issue?"

"Well, you listed 'cautious and not trusting' as a powerful attribute in you. As I said earlier, you weren't born with that one, Bob, quite the opposite. When you were born you were open and trusting and everything was an adventure. But something happened and presto, "cautious and not trusting" appeared in you. Can you see how that can get in the way of relationships and can restrict you in so many ways?"

Bob didn't answer, but he was thinking of the last Board meeting. He was definitely less than forthcoming. As he replayed the meeting in his head he was able to see how he had avoided simple requests for information, and had been defensive when he didn't need to be. Phil had later put him at ease and Bob had then shared what really happened in the field, but he was cautious and not trusting with the other members of the Board. If he were in their shoes he wouldn't have been happy at all. It made him look unsure of himself, or as though he was hiding something.

"Well, right now you are intellectually aware of being cautious and not trusting," said Jack, noticing Bob's apparent state of internal reflection. "Later, if you want, you can let go of the limiting belief underlying that behavior."

As Bob listened, he found himself being more open than he ever thought he would be, but he didn't really understand what Jack could do that would allow him to let go of a non-supportive behavior so easily.

Jack continued to draw Bob out. They explored what Bob loved to do in his personal and professional lives and were able to uncover a wide range of skills, talents and abilities that, again, were so taken for granted they were invisible. Bob saw that he used some of those talents in his work, but not at home and vice versa. That awareness alone made him think about what else he'd been missing.

Jack began to write another subject up on the flip chart, and as he wrote he asked, "So now I want you to describe a time in your life when you were fully using and expressing yourself. When time seemed to stand still and what you were doing felt effortless, a time when you experienced joy and you were totally in the moment."

When Jack was finished writing he stood to the side of the flip chart. He had written the words *Peak Experience*.

It was clear from Bob's body language that he was already there.

"It was 0500 in Iraq during the first war," Bob began. "There was smoke everywhere and the sunrise in front of us was as red as blood mixed

---

Peak Experience

"It was 0500 in Iraq...

with solid black smoke from the oil fires. I'll never forget it. An RPG round slammed into the door of my Humvee and the noise scared the hell out of me. I looked down and saw the round sticking through the door five inches from my hip. I knew it hadn't detonated because I was still alive. The rest happened in slow motion as I jumped out of the vehicle with my radio man, Jeff Harper, and began deploying my men and getting a handle on our situation.

"All hell seemed to break loose, with dirt flying up all over the place. I was in this slow motion time warp where everything was clear and there was no fear. I pointed and my men went there. I spoke and it happened. The entire engagement was over in just a few minutes. The remarkable thing was that we captured 28 combatants without a single casualty and none of the enemy was killed or wounded either. As we sprang into action the enemy's hands just started going up. But then the real surprise happened."

"What was that?" asked Jack.

"Bill Mitchell, an 18 year old kid from Waukon, Iowa brought me a prisoner. God, we were so young. The prisoner's name – he was an officer – was Haulob Fajied, I'll never forget him. He spoke excellent English. I found out later he'd graduated from Boston University just two years before – talk about a small world. He kept insisting he was sorry for the attack and that all he wanted to do was surrender. I didn't understand at first. But then he took us around a bank, and there were 300 more of his soldiers with their weapons on the ground, and their hands in the air waving white t-shirts.

"It turned out the RPG round was fired accidentally by a young conscript who was all of six days in uniform – if you could call it that – and scared shitless. Imagine almost being toast, and then capturing 328 of the enemy and no one gets hurt. That was amazing. Someone was looking out for us that day."

"Boy, I'd say," said Jack. "So Bob, what were you feeling while you were going through this peak experience?"

Sitting back in his chair and looking down, Bob said, "I guess I would have to say I was fully alive. I was aware of everything around me, yet I had no fear. I was fully calm and at peace with myself. I knew exactly what had to be done, and I did it without a lot of thinking or worrying. I moved my arm and the seas parted. It was like that," Bob declared.

"Excellent. And what was important, special or meaningful to you about this experience?" Jack encouraged Bob to go deeper.

Bob took a few minutes to ponder the question.

"I guess it just wasn't my turn to die...that I still had something else to give. I don't know why that RPG round didn't detonate. It's a reliable weapon."

"So what else did it mean to you?" asked Jack.

"I guess it meant that I could trust myself to do the right thing...that I could trust my men to do the right things...and that training pays off."

"Interesting," said Jack. "Where was 'not trusting' during this experience?"

"I don't know. I guess the situation left no room for that. Maybe another one of my core values kicked in, like *natural leader*?" Bob suggested with a big grin on his face.

"One of the key skills you are learning in this process is being aware or 'noticing' what is going on with yourself relative to your values, actions and situations. Observing that one of your core values, 'natural leader' kicked in, is an example of 'noticing'. Now, I have one last question."

"Okay."

"What did you bring to this experience that was uniquely you?"

"Calmness in the face of terror. I've always been that way. The shit hits the fan and I go inside and simply do what needs to be done. On the outside I look like I'm in charge, I suppose, but inside I somehow suspend my mental processes and instinctively make 'it' happen."

Uniquely You

- Confidence
- Self esteem
- Clear away confusion
- Awareness
- Knowing the game

Jack had been recording Bob's thoughts on chart paper while he was sharing his Peak Experience in the form of a story. Jack stepped back from the notes and asked Bob to review them, as well as the notes from their previous discussions. Next, Jack asked Bob to underline any words or phrases that held special meaning or significance for him, or struck an emotional chord for some reason. There were a few words and phrases that stood out for Bob which he underlined. Jack recorded these five sets of words on a new chart sheet.

"Great work, Bob. It's one o'clock so let's go to lunch. The restaurant downstairs is open and they have a pretty broad menu."

As Bob got up to leave he looked around the room. There was chart paper everywhere, from one end of the room to the other. He would have never guessed anyone would be able to get this much out of him in so little time.

CONSIDER

- Intention is the first element of creation. Intention focuses on what we want to happen. The other elements of creation are belief, emotion and action. C=I+B+E+A (Creation = Clear Intention + Positive or Supportive Belief + Positive Emotion + Positive Action).

- Core Values are those attributes you were born with. They are always supportive in nature.

- Learned attributes are either supportive or non-supportive.

- Learned attributes can be as influential as our Core Values.

- Anger and frustration are indications that a Core Value has been violated.

- You can tell if an attribute is learned, rather than a Core Value, if you can violate it when it is convenient and you feel just fine about it.

- Most people are unaware of their Values, and they remain invisible until called into question.

- Each person has a unique set of Values and Learned Attributes.

- Beliefs, and therefore learned attributes and behaviors, can be reinforced, changed or eliminated to assist organizations and individuals in becoming more effective.

- Peak Experiences highlight what it feels like to live our Values, Purpose and Passion

Chapter 11

Timeline Integration

The wounded child in us is real - and more dominant than we know.

Because they chose the buffet they only spent thirty minutes at lunch. As they returned to the Visioning room Jack began, "Bob, we're going to do an exercise that will integrate everything we've done so far. So to begin, I want you to imagine that your timeline on the chart up there is projected on the floor from here to there."

Jack pointed to the floor and then asked Bob, "Where's the beginning of your life, on the right or the left?"

"On the left," said Bob.

"Great," said Jack. "I want you to go to the beginning of your time line. I then want you to walk up the line, knowing everything you now know, and I want you to simply experience your rich and fulfilled life. There is nothing else for you to do but experience whatever you experience. Then, when you get to today, I want you to consider the future and walk to the end of your life. When you get there, just turn around."

Bob was surprised to find himself just going with the flow. He stepped on his imaginary time line, closed his eyes to focus his attention and began to walk slowly forward. As he did so, his entire life came alive. Jack watched him proceed and noticed that his physiology became rigid at the beginning of the line, but softened as he moved forward. Again, when Bob got to what seemed to be the present on the time line, he stopped. There seemed to be a marked hesitation in going forward into the future, with what looked like three false starts. Bob's hands were crossed in front of him. But finally, he seemed to force his hands to his sides and, with his chin out, moved into the future. When Bob got to the end of the line, he turned and just stood there looking down. He seemed to be in a deeply reflective place.

"So how did that go?" Jack asked.

"It was both exhilarating and confusing. Exhilarating because I've done a lot in my life and I have no regrets. There was something, though. A feeling I had early on, like dread. My heart felt so heavy. I don't know what it was, but it felt, well, like dread."

"And what about when you got to the present. What was that about?" asked Jack.

"You saw something?" inquired Bob, a bit surprised.

"Yes, it looked like you had some trouble stepping off into the future," Jack reflected.

"Yes, I had to actually force myself to do it."

"Would you like to know what that was?" asked Jack.

"What do you mean, what that was?"

"Remember the 'cautious and not trusting' learned behavior we were talking about earlier?" reminded Jack.

Bob seemed perplexed.

Jack pointed to the 'Non-supportive Learned Attributes' sheet and Bob immediately got the connection.

Jack continued, "Based on your body language early on the time line, and from what you shared with me this morning, I would guess that 'cautious and not trusting' got its start early on in your life. This learned behavior clearly no longer serves you. Rather, it's keeping you from moving freely into the future with your full power. Does that make any sense to you?"

"It does," shared Bob slowly, "but how can you be sure?"

"Well, among other things, Bob, I've been trained to work with limiting beliefs and the limiting behaviors they cause," Jack replied. "So, if you want to see what caused 'cautious and not trusting,' we can easily do that. And if you decide to let it go, you can do that as well. It will only take a few minutes and you'll be able to tell instantly if the barrier is removed."

Bob felt very uncomfortable. He began to feel this was a stupid exercise. He closed his eyes again and took a deep breath and found himself thinking as he had earlier in the morning, "Move forward? Stay where I am? Trust the process? Leave now?" He took another deep breath. Bob's eyes opened wide and he said out loud "No! I don't think so," stood up and walked toward the door.

"Okay, said Jack, "I understand. But before you make up your mind completely, may I tell you more about how limiting beliefs and behaviors begin to form at an early age? Would you be willing to just listen while I explain?"

Bob stopped his progress toward the door and leaned against the wall. Jack knew that he was talking directly to that part of Bob that was "cautious and not trusting." If Jack appealed to this part of Bob by outlining what to expect, chances were that part of Bob would be willing to participate.

"Well, sure, go ahead," Bob agreed, somewhat surprised at his answer.

"All right then," said Jack. "Have you ever in your life felt that part of you wanted to do something and, at the same time, part of you didn't?" Jack questioned.

"You mean like now?" asked Bob, with a chagrined look on his face.

"Yes. And that's the point. Part of you is cautious for some reason, but for what reason? What we know now is that your cautiousness is more deeply protective of you than maybe you ever knew. There was a belief created at some point in your young life by some event which you had neither the experience nor the skills to handle. As a very young child you instantly, and probably even unconsciously, made up your mind that you'd never let down your guard again," Jack explained.

"How young was I?" Bob thought back.

"Oh, probably between two and ten years old," Jack replied. "But listen," Jack continued, "I want that part of you we are calling 'cautious and not trusting' to know that there is nothing wrong. In fact that part of you has been working hard protecting you all these years. All we want to do right now is to acknowledge, appreciate, and try to understand how this part came to support you in the way that it does. Once you understand what happened, you'll have the choice to use 'cautious and not trusting' or not. Right now, however, you aren't experiencing choice; you respond with an automatic reaction to anything new or seemingly threatening. Going forward, you can begin to put 'not trusting' into a new perspective and give it a more positive role."

"Like your choosing not to use that 4-letter word in the Navy," joked Bob.

"Yes, exactly like that," said Jack.

Bob took a tentative step toward Jack and said, "Okay, what do I do to let go of this cautiousness?"

"Well, remember the time line?" Jack pointed to the floor.

"Yes," Bob followed.

"Well get back on the time line at today, facing the future."

"Okay," Bob complied, walking half way up the imaginary line and closing his eyes.

Letting Go of What Stops You

"I want you to recall that feeling of dread that you spoke of earlier. Can you?" Jack asked.

"I have it," said Bob, holding his right hand over his heart and rubbing it. "It's definitely with me."

"Have you experienced this feeling in your chest before?" Jack asked.

"Yes, but until this minute I didn't realize how much or for how long it's been with me." It had been with him off and on throughout the morning and Bob remembered the last time he was aware of it was two days before, at the recent Board meeting.

"What I want you to do is slowly move backwards on your time line and tell me when that feeling disappears," Jack directed.

"Just go backward until it disappears!" Bob repeated, looking at Jack with some disbelief.

"Yes. Do that now. Take as much time as you need," Jack encouraged him.

Bob bowed his head again, and looked down at the imaginary line he was standing on. He began to step backward toward his childhood.

As he got closer to the beginning of his life, he stopped and said the feeling was still there. Jack told him to just keep backing down the line. A few more steps and Jack noticed the dramatic release of tension in Bob.

"It's gone," said Bob with a look of some amusement on his face.

"Good. Now I want you to step forward on the line until the feeling comes back," Jack directed.

Bob stepped forward and his body changed to show some heavy burden.

"You have the feeling of dread again?"

"Yes," said Bob.

"Where are you?" asked Jack.

"I'm in the den at our house in Texas," Bob answered, surprised at how sure the words were.

"How old are you." Jack continued with his questions and Bob answered.

"Six. It's Christmas Day."

"Is there anyone else with you?"

"My dad. He's sleeping on the couch."

"What's happening?"

"Nothing – I don't know what happened – I didn't do anything," Bob said defensively, tears suddenly welling up in his eyes and his head falling forward.

"Why are you there?"

"Mom sent me in to wake Dad up for Christmas dinner. Everyone was ready."

"What's happening, Bob?" asked Jack quietly.

"He's not waking up. I'm shaking his hand and he is really cold. I'm yelling at him and shaking him to wake up but he's not waking up."

"Okay. Bob, I want you to listen to me," speaking more firmly, "Step off the line. Do it now, Bob!"

Bob stepped off the invisible line. He stood there bent over with his hands on his hips shaking his head back and forth. He then stood upright and tilted his head back so he could look up and stem the tears and the obvious emotion.

"You're okay now," said Jack, with his hand on Bob's shoulder.

After a moment Bob said, "I'm sorry. I don't know what happened just then. I haven't thought about that for almost thirty years."

"That's all right," said Jack. "Quite a trauma for a six-year-old boy to have to go through, isn't it?

"Yes, it is."

"So, Bob, are you willing to help this young child let go of this feeling, this 'cautious' and 'not trusting'?" Jack asked.

"Yes."

"Are you sure you are ready?"

"Yes."

"OK, step back on the line,' Jack directed.

As Bob did so, the tears welled up again. His head was bent toward the floor and his eyes were closed.

"Can you see your six year old self there, amid all the hurt and pain and confusion?"

"Yes," Bob replied.

"What is he making this all mean, Bob? What does all this hurt and pain and confusion mean to this six year old child?" asked Jack.

"That – that he had something to do with Dad dying. That he had no control. That he could never fully trust – himself again."

"And is that belief the truth?" Jack offered.

"No, of course not, the doctors said he died in his sleep at least two hours before of a massive heart attack. I had nothing whatsoever to do with Dad dying," Bob said raising his head.

"But your six-year-old self believes otherwise, doesn't he?" Jack suggested.

"Yes," Bob answered, lowering his head again.

"If you were to say something to this young boy that could make the biggest difference in his young life right now, what would that be?" Jack coached.

"That it's going to be alright. That it's not his fault. That Dad loves him and that God just called Dad home to heaven," Bob said, head upright.

"What else would you tell him?" Jack continued.

"That I love him," Bob whispered.

"Excellent, Bob, I want you to bend down and take his hand in yours, and I want you to tell him that."

Bob looked at Jack, skepticism rising, and feeling more than a little stupid and ridiculous.

Jack motioned for him to go ahead. "Do it Bob, this is as real as life ever gets, right here and right now. Your mind can't tell the difference and you need to let this go."

Bob got down on his knee, closed his eyes and looked into his six-year-old self's eyes and told him, "It's going to be alright, Bobby. It's not your fault. Dad loves you. All that happened was God called Dad home to heaven. Bobby, I love you. And we are going to be okay. There is nothing to be afraid of."

"How does your six-year-old self feel now?" Jack asked

"He feels better. Not as afraid. He feels safe," Bob realized.

"Good. Now, still holding him by the hand, I want you to tell him that you know that he has been working really hard to protect you all these years. I want you to thank him and tell him it's okay and that he can let go and you will take it from here. Do that now," Jack directed.

Still feeling somewhat foolish and self conscious, Bob did so.

"Now, I want you to walk with him through your life up to today. And, as you walk I want your 39 year old self to be aware of all the ways 'cautious' and 'not trusting' has kept you from being fully self expressed. Yet, at the same time, I want you to realize that it was all okay, that every unique experience has led perfectly to bring you to where you are today. Do you understand?"

"Yes."

"Then go."

Bob stood, and holding his six year old self's hand, slowly walked the imaginary time line to the present. When he got to the end of the line, Jack said, "Look at your six-year-old self now, how old is he?"

"He's my age."

"Good, excellent. Put your arms around him and draw him into you once and for all."

Still feeling somewhat ridiculous, yet at the same time at peace,

Bob put his arms out and hugged that small boy.

Bob was exhausted. He sat down, closed his eyes, put his head back and took a few deep breaths. After a few minutes Jack asked again, "So, how are you now?"

"I know that I have never done anything like this in my life. It was very strange. Like I was really myself at six and my current self all at once," he said with a note of wonderment in his voice. "I don't remember ever doing anything so powerful," Bob confessed. "It was like really being there."

"You were," said Jack. "You were really that six year old and you really were in that place with your father. And for over thirty three years, your six-year-old self was working hard to protect you from any future pain or fear of uninvited surprise. At some point, however, that protection was no longer useful. In fact, this protection began to get in the way, but because it was forgotten and invisible, it continued to affect your life. What we just did was to fully acknowledge and appreciate the pain that six-year-old felt and set him free to grow up."

Bob just stood there, unmoving, in a kind of a daze. Jack broke in suggesting, "Let's take a break, Bob."

Jack's office bordered a park, so Jack suggested Bob go for a walk.

As Bob began his stroll, he began to notice his surroundings. Everything seemed so vibrant – the grass, the green pine trees, the blue sky and the smell of honeysuckle in the air. Bob found himself feeling strangely alive and vital, like he had felt in Iraq all those years ago, only without the mortal danger. He began to review what he just experienced and was amazed that he had lived with the burden of this limiting belief for all those years, and then, in just a few minutes, he could feel so free from it. How many of the people at CI were suffering from unconscious barriers of their own? How much had this invisible issue really affected his life and the company? He was eager to finish up the day and see where it would lead..

CREATING THE FUTURE

"Remember in our first telephone conversation, I asked you if you would like to be able to *design the future rather than simply react to it*, and if you would like to be able to *intend something and have it happen*. Do you remember that?"

"Yeah, and I asked if you were some kind of wizard."

"You noticed I didn't laugh, didn't you? So, what you're going to do is what we call 'future pace' to make sure 'cautious' and 'not trusting' are no longer dominant and you have authentic choice. Are you ready?"

"Yes."

"Good, now I want you to close your eyes again and relax. Imagine it's some time in the future. I want you to imagine a situation that, in the past, would have made you, 'cautious and not trusting.' Let me know when you have one," Jack requested.

Bob thought about the Board meeting he'd experienced a few days ago in San Francisco, and about the Board meeting he would be having at the end of next week.

"Okay," said Bob, "I'm in that situation."

"How are you feeling?" Jack checked.

"I'm feeling great. Right now I have no dread in my heart. No 'cautious' and no 'not trusting'. I'm just open to whatever happens. I can take care of myself so I can afford to trust, to have faith that everything will turn out all right."

"Okay. Now Bob, I want you to form a clear intention for what you want to have happen at that future event." Jack allowed Bob time to visualize this event and then asked, "How do you intend it to go?"

"Well, what I first thought about was the last Board meeting and how badly it went. So my 'future pace' is the meeting I'll be having with them at the end of next week. In my future pace I feel confident and self-assured. Open and looking forward to what the Board wants to contribute. For my next meeting I intend to engage the Board in helping me create a new future for the company, and I plan to have fun doing it," said Bob, relaxing into the chair with a smile on his face.

After a pause Bob looked at Jack and said, "Thank you, Jack. That was amazing." Jack smiled at Bob. "You're welcome."

CONSIDER

- Non-supportive Limiting Beliefs are the root cause of non-supportive behaviors.

- Letting go of what stops us requires uncovering the underlying belief.

- When we change our beliefs, we change our world.

- The first step to changing beliefs is to be aware they exist.

- Future pacing allows us to prepare our inner resources to face any kind of challenge in advance. Future pacing is simply practicing for the event as a positive, supportive outcome.

CHAPTER 12

PASSION & PURPOSE

"Without Vision, the People Perish."
– God

Jack said, "I want to introduce you to what we simply call *The Human Model* of existence. I am not introducing this as a truth, but simply as a model we can use for discussion. Is that okay with you?"

"Sure," said Bob.

"Good. So far we've looked at your life from a number of different perspectives and what's not on the walls is at least in your awareness. We've talked about your personality, uncovered your Core Values, and briefly looked at how supportive and non-supportive beliefs affect your behavior. We've looked at your unique abilities and identified many skills, talents and abilities. These are the guiding and enabling parts of our human model. They exist to support your Purpose and Passion, which are the next parts that we will uncover and articulate.

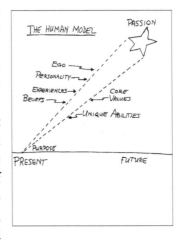

I'm going to give you some steps to follow but then it will be up to you. I'll be here for you as a sounding board and coach. Are you ready?" asked Jack.

"Let's see where this goes," said Bob with more enthusiasm than he had shown all day.

Jack explained that Bob's Purpose and Passion statement would be comprised of two elements. The first part would be his Purpose and the second part would be his Passion.

"Your Purpose is what you bring to life simply by being in it. It occurs in the present moment. Your Purpose is what you bring to everything and every role you play in life. You are not your role, Bob, but what you bring to the role. Does that make sense?"

"A little. I really don't know where to begin," replied Bob. "Can you give me a hint?"

"Sure. I can give you some structure but remember, whatever form your Purpose statement takes is secondary to whether or not the words speak to you. While many use the format I'm going to share with you, some simply write a poem that speaks to them. So use what I give you only as an example, okay?"

"Okay, I understand."

"One of the first things you will want to do is begin to describe how you address the world. Pick two or three words that describe how you address the world."

"Can you give me an example?"

"Sure, would you mind if I shared my Purpose Statement with you?"

"That would be great."

> **People at Peace with Themselves & Others**
>
> Through Intimacy & Sharing, I help myself and others appreciate our pasts, be courageously engaged in the present, and excited about our futures

Jack wrote his Purpose and Passion Statement on the chart and recited it out loud.

"As you can see, there are two parts. The first part is my Purpose statement on the bottom. It begins 'Through intimacy and sharing…' These are the two words that best describe how I engage the world."

"You think?" laughed Bob.

Jack just smiled, "Other people have had three or four words, but all that matters is that *the words you choose speak to you*. In my experience, if they speak to you others will recognize them in you."

"The next word in the statement is pretty special as well. I use the word *help*. Others use words like *teach, inspire, lead*, etc. Pick a word that describes your style. After that, well, just write what you think you're here to do."

"Okay," acknowledged Bob. "So that's your Purpose

Statement," he said, pointing to the statement beginning with *Through Intimacy and Sharing*...I'm beginning to understand – to get a sense of how I can write that, but I don't understand what your Passion statement means. Here you have '*People at Peace with Themselves and Others.*' How is your Passion statement related to your Purpose?" questioned Bob.

"Really good question. If Purpose occurs in the moment, then Passion is in the future, it's my legacy. As I fulfill my Purpose, I believe that I am giving my life so that we can be at peace with ourselves and ultimately, find it easier to be at peace with others. To keep it memorable, I've shortened all that to *People at Peace with Themselves and Others*. These simple words have profound meaning for me, Bob, and I'm privileged to live them every day in the work that I do."

"Yes, I can clearly see that," shared Bob.

"Thank you, Bob. Listen, I'm going to leave you alone for a few minutes with your thoughts. As you begin to think about your Purpose, don't forget to refer to all the words you underlined earlier. They hold clues for you to consider. I'll be right out here if you get stuck."

Bob, already writing on a blank sheet of chart paper simply nodded.

Twenty minutes later Bob stood in front of the flip chart and read the words that had flowed easily out of him. Bob was amazed at how energized he was. As he read the words for the second time they spoke to him like his own DNA. They were as familiar as his name, yet he was looking at them for the first time. He knew these words reflected both who he was in the moment – and what his potential was in the future: his Purpose and Passion. He called Jack into the room.

Jack came in, sat down and read Bob's Passion and Purpose Statement out loud. He smiled. "So, Bob, on a scale of 1-10, with

> **Confidence & Self Esteem**
>
> With clarity of focus and relentless caring, I inspire
> myself and others to rise above the chaos, have faith in one another, and risk taking the kind of action that makes a difference in the world.

10 being completely, how close is this statement to capturing the essential Bob Harris?"

"It's a 10," said Bob, with a big smile on his face.

Jack stood and walked over and shook Bob's hand. "It's a pleasure to meet you, Bob Harris. Why don't you sign and date it," Jack invited.

"Thanks, Jack. This has been an amazing day!" Bob put his signature on a piece of paper that meant more to him than anything else he had ever signed.

"Let's take a break, and when we come back I want to look at the implications of knowing who you really are." smiled Jack.

When the two men returned from a brisk walk around the complex they got right back to it.

"Life's Passion – some say Joy – is in fulfilling one's Purpose," stated Jack.

Bob thought about it for a moment and then answered, "I can see that, Jack, I really can."

"Good work," said Jack.

"I am going to introduce you to what we call the *EP Model*, and I'd like you to try it on and see if it makes sense to you." said Jack as he partially flipped to a page he had finished earlier. But he stood there for a minute thinking. Then he walked away from the flip chart pad without fully unfolding the new page.

He sat in front of Bob and began "I believe we are all born with Ego and Purpose," extending both arms, his hands in fists in front of him, "and that they were meant to work together in order for us to be fulfilled in this life. Our Ego, on one hand, is an important part of our default operating system responsible for protecting our physical and psychological selves. The Ego's nature is to look for what's wrong or dangerous and keep us safe, mostly by maintaining the status quo. *Cautious and not trusting* is an amplified part of your Ego-self. The Ego doesn't want you to change nor does it want anyone or anything around you to change either.

"Our Purpose, on the other hand, is meant to inspire and guide our Ego-selves in fulfillment of our unique Passion. In fact the key to our Passion lies in fulfilling our Purpose.

"Your Passion, for example, is to bring Confidence and Self Esteem to the world around you. Said another way, you are the possibility of confidence and self esteem in the world. And there is great joy for you in being that. But the only path to confidence and self esteem is through your Purpose. You must, from this moment on, act with *clarity of focus and relentless caring to inspire yourself and others to rise above the chaos, have faith in one another and risk taking the kind of action that makes a difference in the world.*

"What you've just created is a new context for your life, Bob. In this simple statement you are moving from a 'human doing' to a 'human being.' And this is only the beginning. So, let's look at the implications of what you've said.

"What does *clarity of focus*, mean to you?"

"Well," said Bob, fully engaged in the question, "it refers not only to where I'm going and what I want, but also, to identifying and changing the limiting beliefs that can get in the way of it."

"Excellent," said Jack. "And what does *relentless caring* mean to you?"

Clarity of Focus	Being clear about what I want. Also includes uncovering personal and organizational limiting beliefs that might get in the way of what I want. Being aware, being open
Relentless Caring	Having respect for all people, no matter what the circumstance
Inspire	Where people act out of their heart. They act because something is important to them
Rise above the Chaos	This describes the reactive environment we live in and our ability to do more of the things that matter to our Purpose
Have Faith in one another	Faith in humanity to want to do the right thing
Risk taking action	Let go of our fear and act anyway. Be courageous
that makes a difference in the world	I think getting results are different than making a difference. Results are different than doing what's important. I don't want to make a profit, for example, if I have to damage the environment

Over the next half hour Bob defined each part of his Passion and Purpose statement, and with each definition he felt more clarity and passion about the possibility.

When they were done both men just sat there for a moment and looked at the work they had accomplished together. Jack then stood and faced Bob and said, "I won't kid you Bob, it's not going to be easy being you. What follows will require you 'being' your Purpose and Core Values in everything you do. It will require that you practice *mastery of self*. But when you do, you'll experience the joy of bringing *Confidence & Self Esteem* to yourself and others.

"I understand," said Jack.

"In the past, you've unconsciously expressed your Purpose and Core Values and experienced your Passion in those moments when you've felt most fulfilled. Iraq was a big one for you.

"So, Bob," finished Jack, "who you are is what you bring to life simply by being in it. You're not your business card, nor any of the roles you play. You are not your possessions, your family, your beliefs or even your body. *Who you are is what you bring to these things.* And now you are being asked to bring yourself – your Values, Purpose and Passion – to a new role, that of CEO."

"Thanks Jack, I profoundly get that," said Bob. And I will continue to expand the meaning of my Purpose. But can you clear something up for me?"

"Sure," said Bob.

"What is the default operating system you mentioned earlier?"

DEFAULT OPERATING SYSTEM

"Our default operating system is what runs us long before we're aware we have one. Our reactive identity pretty much dominates who we are. Without clear knowledge of our Purpose, there is little free choice, and our responses to life are simply a reaction – automatic, mostly invisible and dominant – although much of it can be changed by the user if they ever knew it existed.

"For simplicity's sake, I'm going to represent our personal operating system as two interacting programs.

- Reactive Identity
- Creative Identity

"Our *Reactive Identity* is made up of our Ego, personality, defining experience, beliefs and learned behaviors and comprises our default operating system.

"Our *Creative Identity* is made up of our Purpose, Passion, Core Values and Unique Abilities and expands the system significantly."

Reactive Identity (Ego-self)	Creative Identity (Purpose-self)
- Ego - Personality - Defining experiences - Beliefs - Learned behaviors	- Purpose - Passion - Core Values - Unique Abilities

"Is this making any sense?" queried Jack.

"Yes, absolutely," said Bob.

"Good, because our *Reactive Identity* – we commonly call it our *Ego-self* – is that part of the human model recognized and celebrated in the world, and so it's become the dominant part of who we are to the detriment of our individual Purpose.

"Now, because our reactive and creative identities have not been distinguished, they are pretty much

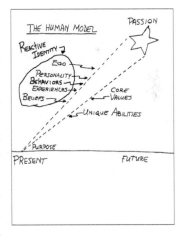

invisible to us, we seldom consider them until and unless they are called into question, just like we have been doing today. We behave like we behave and we say *that's just the way I am.* But what if that isn't just the way we are? What if we were able to scroll down to 'preferences' and discover the full possibility of ourselves just waiting to be brought forward?"

"Well, I guess you'd first have to be aware that there was a preferences function," Bob continued the analogy.

"Absolutely," said Jack.

EGO & PURPOSE

"Real choice occurs only when we're aware of the distinctions *Ego-self and Purpose*. Until then, we are pretty much stuck in the automatic reaction of Ego.

"Because we live in a duality, where everything has an opposite, acting with only Ego is like trying to take on the world with one hand tied behind our back. *And the one hand we're using has the mental ability and experience of a five year old!* We live in an eye-for-an-eye world where humanity is seemingly unconscious to the possibility of who we really are. And so are the organizations we create."

"Our Egos made both of us amazing fire-fighters, Bob, but guided by our Purpose & Passion we can also be amazing leaders."

Bob sat in a trance, thinking about the implications of what Jack was saying. "What if he's right? What kind of energy is waiting to be unleashed, not only in me, but in all of my people?"

"Let's look at the EP chart now. But before we do, I want to remind you about not believing a word I say," Jack said.

Bob smiled and said, "Don't worry; I've been keeping you honest."

"Good, because what I am about to share with you isn't *the* truth. What I want you to do is see if it fits with your experience. Okay?"

Bob nodded "yes" and Jack walked back to the chart he had abandoned earlier.

"What distinguishes an authentic leader from other people is the awareness of and the ability to *choose between* his or her Ego-self and Purpose and Passion *in the moment.*"

"Consider that our Ego-self is reactive, automatic, invisible and driven by fear, uncertainty and doubt. It looks for what's wrong and tries to fix and control everything to maintain the status quo to keep us safe. Its focus in the present is based on the past. The Ego's function is protecting our physical and psychological form from what it perceives we don't want. The world and our organizations are run by a collective Ego that focuses on what we don't want as well."

Bob began to shift uncomfortably in his chair. "Go on," he said.

"Our Purpose, however, is creative, considered and inspired by what's possible. It focuses in the present based on possibilities in the future, and doesn't create drama by making up stories."

"We created this chart to help us distinguish Ego and Purpose more fully," said Jack as he finally pulled the chart over.

Ego Self	Purpose & Passion
- Automatic	- Considered
- Reactive	- Creative
- Operates in Present from Past	- Operates in Present from Future
- Driven by Fear, Uncertainty & Doubt	- Fueled by what's Possible
- Focused on what we don't want	- Focused on what we do want
- Based on our experience & beliefs	- Based on intention and intuition
- Closed & rigid to new ideas	- Open & flexible
- Expends physical energy	- Generates physical energy
- Concerned with Perfection	- Is about making Progress
- Fosters Complaint	- Fosters Solutions
- Requires Trust (Past Experience)	- Bestows Faith from nothing
- Judgmental based upon individual and cultural beliefs held as the truth	- Accepts differences in individual and cultural beliefs
- Separates people by creating fear	- Brings people together in peace
- Strives to keep the status quo	- Desires to expand and create
- At the effect of the world	- Is witness and, cause in the world
- Requires people to act out of circumstance	- Inspires people to act out of love

"What do you mean by making up stories?" asked Bob.

Jack took a moment, and then said, "When my youngest daughter was a teenager she didn't come home when she was supposed to. After one hour I was angry, at two I was worried and at three I was already thinking she was dead along the side of the road somewhere, the victim of the most heinous crime. I was beside myself. Then I saw the note she left for me on my dresser. She was staying with her mother for the weekend."

"I see what you mean," said Bob.

"Purpose always seeks growth, expansion, contribution and keeps our focus on what we intend to create in the world. It is a very positive force.

"Are you still with me, Bob?" Jack asked.

"I'm not completely sure yet, but it's getting clearer," said Bob.

Jack continued, "I want to be very clear here, Bob, there is nothing wrong with our Ego-self. It's essential at protecting our physical form. However it's incomplete without our Purpose. Without the clarity of Purpose our Ego makes up the most chilling scenarios for us to react to. Everything is a drama. That's the message here. If we can distinguish Ego and Purpose we get access to what free choice really is: being conscious of the distinction, and having the ability to choose between these two energies." Jack explained as he pointed to the EP Chart.

The two went through the distinction Ego-self and compared and contrasted it with Purpose. Finally, Jack pointed to the last line on the chart and said, "What we're going to do tomorrow is to distinguish when to manage and when to lead – because they are very distinct energies. One energy, *requiring*, is force from outside of us, like the carrot and the stick, alternately pulling and pushing us to compliance, and there is a time and a place for that. The other energy, *inspiring*, is accessing Power from inside of us – we call it Passion – unleashing authentic desire in the individual. Understand?" sought Jack.

"Yes, I think I am getting it, although I'm still working on the part about Ego and Purpose," Bob said.

"Good. Okay. Tell me what you think I just tried to explain," Jack backtracked.

"That as human beings, we have both Ego and Purpose. Culturally, we are unaware of our Purpose and so we automatically revert to our Ego, which is generally run by fear, uncertainty and doubt. When we finally come to know our true Purpose, we then experience choice and have the ability to choose to live more from our Purpose than our Ego. We understand that Purpose is our contribution to humanity, or our legacy. You said earlier that the real issue is the imbalance, not that one is better than the other. They are both necessary. What's perfect is balance between the two," Bob summed it up.

"How do you know you are coming from your Ego?" Jack checked.

"When there is fear, uncertainty or doubt, when there are judgments and evaluations and looking for what's wrong, when I am referencing the past and – when I have this pressure around my heart."

"Great understanding, Bob! Now, how do you know you are coming from Purpose & Passion?"

"Well, when there is no fear, uncertainty or doubt, I feel at ease in my own skin, at peace with myself. I feel self-confident and open, and know that I am okay, even when someone is going nuts around me," Bob decided.

"Very well put. When you are being who you are meant to be there is no fear. Just like when you were in the war," Jack concluded. "Now, can you give me a recent real life example of when your Ego got the best of you?"

"Yes. Well, not in the way I would have ordinarily recognized or been aware of before today. In the past when I thought of the word Ego I typically thought of strong, forceful characters full of confidence. But in the 'future pace' exercise you had me do earlier it was the opposite. My Ego, supported by the experience of 'cautious and not trusting' was fearful and caused me to act like an idiot at the Board meeting. I was unnecessarily defensive and evasive when I could have been open and engaging. I can see that now. My Purpose wasn't even in the conversation."

"Excellent noticing," reinforced Jack.

HOMEWORK

"Before we complete our day I have some homework for you," said Jack, "a question for you to consider tonight. What corporate limiting beliefs do you, your VP's or the organization have right now?"

"Can you give me an example of a corporate limiting belief," asked Bob.

"Sure. Essentially, limiting beliefs are beliefs people and organizations have about themselves and each other that no longer serve them. An example would be: People never change. Another would be: Management doesn't care about us. Or, if we reference the individual," said Jack, pointing to the Values sheet hanging on the wall, "we see cautious and not trusting from this morning. Get the picture?"

"Yes," said Bob, who already had a couple more bouncing around in his head. He was sure there would be a few more.

CLEARING

"Just as we did a Clearing when we started the day, it's important to bring some closure to this session with another clearing process. What were some of the highlights for you – was there anything you wish I'd done differently – and is there anything you'd like to say to be complete with the day?" Jack asked.

Bob sat back in the chair and stared up at the ceiling. Speaking mostly to himself, he said, "It was like nothing I ever expected. Intense at times, but surprisingly, I feel refreshed. Although I found myself resisting some of your comments, I did like the exercises you put me through. For the first time that I can ever remember, I got a good look at who I was meant to be. Knowing this about myself is exciting because I know I have an opportunity, even an obligation, to make a difference in a lot of people's lives. That's meaningful

---

Intentions

1. Integrate PDQ quickly into the rest of the company
2. Get our leadership leading instead of fighting
3. Reduce expenses and improve throughput and sales revenue
4. Learn more about myself and my leadership style
5. Learn to be an effective CEO faster than I would on my own
6. Quickly tie what I learn here into results for the organization
7. Discover some useful things about my people I'm not seeing yet

to me, and something I didn't really know I wanted to do until today."

Bob shifted his gaze from the ceiling and looked at Jack. "I recall you said my life would dramatically change by the end of the day. I don't know if I believe that yet, Jack, but looking at my Purpose & Passion statement I see that the potential is there. I'm concerned about how to hold on to this feeling of Purpose and level of clarity once I leave your office and re-enter the other 'real world.'"

"That's understandable," replied Jack. We will address sustainability tomorrow. In the meantime, let's look at your intentions from this morning. What have we accomplished from there?" asked Jack as he pointed to the appropriate sheet.

"Definitely number four, but also a ton of insight into the rest as well. I expect we will address them tomorrow?"

"Absolutely," reassured Jack.

Bob sat still for a few minutes. He had a smile on his face.

"So is there anything else you need to say to complete today?" asked Jack.

"Yes. Thanks Jack. I mean it, really. Today was meaningful. I can't wait to call Phil and thank him for kicking me in the ass to get here. I really owe him a debt of gratitude. And, well, I know I can sometimes be a bit mulish when I don't agree or understand. So, hey, thanks for encouraging me get to my own understanding and acceptance with all of this without pushing or pulling me."

"You're welcome," replied Jack as the two men shook hands.

With notes in hand, Bob left the office and walked back to the Hyatt. It was a beautiful night and the air had a damp and cool scent of flowers and freshly cut grass.

CONSIDER

- Human Beings are born with Ego and Purpose, and until these two are joined, the exponential power of Purpose & Passion remains buried inside.

- To leverage organizations in the future, we must liberate the untapped power held in each individual.

- You know you are dealing from Ego when there seems to be something wrong that needs fixing, and you feel stress. You focus on changing wrongs from the past. There is fear, uncertainty or doubt.

- You know you are dealing from Purpose when you experience clarity, alignment, peace, confidence and fun. You realize that you cannot change the past so you begin by changing in the moment.

- Powerful leadership occurs when you are able to choose between acting from the past or from the future. The most powerful choices in life and in business occur once you are aware of the duality of Ego and Purpose.

- Ego is not inherently bad, but Ego without the guidance of Purpose causes a lot of mischief. We were intended to work with a balance.

- We all have moments when we are fully alive and expressing ourselves. These are called Peak Experiences. We regard them as accidental. They are not. They are how we were meant to be.

CHAPTER 13

ENCOURAGEMENT

*The only limit to our realization of tomorrow
will be our doubts of today.*
— Franklin D. Roosevelt

When Bob returned to his room after working out he felt restless, yet at the same time strangely at peace. Whenever he traveled he and Linda always talked by phone – and tonight was no exception. After the usual exchange about the kids and household issues, Bob fell uncharacteristically silent when Linda asked him about his day. He hardly knew where to begin his explanation, but started in by saying, "My day was like nothing I've experienced or done before. This guy, Jack, worked with me to, I guess, help me sort out who I am and what and how I want to be in this new CEO job."

Linda listened with curiosity, hearing something like wonder and at the same time, hesitancy, in Bob's voice. He shared the day with her, describing the various exercises Jack led him through to discover his Core Values and Limiting Beliefs. He even told her about the bizarre timeline process when Jack had him talking to his six-year-old self when his father died.

"It's somewhat complicated and difficult to describe how it all happened, but I'm going to read you something that pretty well sums up the work I did with Jack. It's going to sound pretty woo-woo, so don't laugh, okay?" Bob looked down at his notes from the day and read his Purpose & Passion statement to Linda.

"My Passion, or in the end, what I am living my life for, is to bring Confidence & Self Esteem to the world.

"My Purpose is: With clarity of focus and relentless caring, I inspire myself and others to rise above the chaos, have faith in one another, and risk taking the kind of action that makes a difference in the world."

Although Bob was a little unsure of what Linda's reaction might be, he felt safe enough sharing this with her. She was the one person in the world whom he absolutely trusted and with whom he shared his inner thoughts. At the end of his reading she was silent, then quietly said, "Wow."

"Wow?"

"Yeah, wow. I am so impressed – and actually proud – that you would be willing to do something like this. As your wife and biggest fan, I already know these things about you. But it must have felt really risky for you to be this open with a perfect stranger – for you to engage in this 'touchy-feely' stuff?"

"Yes, it all seemed that way at the beginning of the day, and I actually thought that some of what Jack asked me to do was full of nonsense," Bob acknowledged. "But at some point I thought, what the heck, just go with it, and I'm glad I did."

"Me too," replied Linda. "I've always thought you would be a great guy to work for – and if you put this spin on your already great self – the company will really be lucky to have you as their CEO."

Bob smiled to himself. He was the lucky guy to have someone like Linda in his corner.

The conversation shifted back to the home front, and as they said their goodbyes Linda told Bob she was looking forward to hearing from him tomorrow

Bob slept well and woke up refreshed and eager to work with Jack. As he was shaving he really looked at himself and reflected on his true passion: *helping others build confidence and self esteem in themselves.* He tried to imagine Corporate Insights full of confident people, people who believed in themselves and each other instead of exhibiting all the self-doubt, backstabbing and infighting. What kind of success could they build together if this could be changed? Bob was excited about the possibility of building a powerful support structure to instill a strong sense of leadership in each of his people. He was looking forward to finding out what Jack had planned for the day.

CHAPTER 14

VISIONING DAY TWO

CREATING A GAME WORTH PLAYING

"What would you attempt if you knew you would not fail?"
– Dr. Robert Schuller

After another brisk walk from the Hotel Bob stopped to watch the ducks again before entering the office. Jack saw him standing at the railing and went out to greet him.

"Good morning, Bob. I just made a fresh pot of coffee," Jack offered, "I'm afraid we're on our own today. Beverly is out hiking with her nieces who are visiting from Buffalo." The two men walked back to the Visioning room with a diversion to the perking coffee.

Bob had been amazed at the service Beverly had provided on Friday. From her initial introduction to whenever refreshment was needed, she seemed to anticipate everything.

"You know Jack, if I didn't mention it already, I just wanted you to know how impressed I am with who Beverly is. Hell, she pitches your company better than you do."

Jack laughed and said, "She'll be pleased to hear that! She's relentless already."

Bob fetched his own coffee from the kitchen. When he came back, Jack was standing next to the chart. After Clearing, Bob took a sip of his coffee and Jack began.

"Remember our second phone call?"

"Sort of," said Bob.

"Well, it was then that I guaranteed that in 90 days you could have a newly aligned and engaged organization. I also said that that would just be the beginning. That although we could get your leadership and management team and the rest of the organization fully engaged in 90 days, it would be up to you to *keep* them engaged."

"And that's when you gave me your definition of engaged," remembered Bob.

"Yes, I did. I said that engaged means that everyone in the organization feels *challenged, appreciated, personally responsible and part of a game they feel is worth playing* – a game that inspires them.

Engaged means you feel

- Challenged
- Appreciated
- Responsible for the Outcome
- Part of a Game worth playing

"As part of our work we're doing, we have a process to share with you that will assist you in fully engaging people. So our job today is threefold.

"First, you will articulate exactly what you want from the company in terms of behavior and results in mission critical areas in, say, six months. This will be a one-man strategic planning session.

"Second, you will articulate an inspiring organizational Vision that you're excited to share with the Board and your people. This Vision, when explored for its implications will both engage and inspire your Board and employees as well.

How to Engage Corporate Insights

1. Articulate exactly what you want
2. Articulate an inspiring Corporate Vision
3. Approve a Transformational Process

"And lastly, if you agree of course, you will approve a transformational process that will bring all of your people:

- to a new level of self-awareness
- into full alignment with your Vision
- and engage them fully in achieving the goals necessary to achieve your Vision in the desired time frame.

"Is this what you want?"

"Sure, Jack. Who wouldn't want something like that – and all accomplished in one day! I have to tell you, though; I'm feeling somewhat skeptical again. It seems like a big undertaking, but I'm in your hands and ready to go for it. Since I'll be meeting with the

Board again when I get back, I'm especially motivated to have something substantial to show them. Hopefully I'll be better prepared than I was the other day."

"You'll knock their socks off, not to worry," affirmed Jack, more animated than Bob had seen him before. "I think it appropriate that we begin our day with a discussion about creating positive change in organizations. After all, as I believe I mentioned earlier, you will only have five quarters to realign the company behind a new Vision of the future. Take any longer than that and you will probably be on your way to trouble with the Board."

"Five quarters, how about five weeks?" commented Bob, recalling his first Board meeting.

Jack smiled. "Again, Bob, no problem. Over the course of the next hour or so I'm going to give you a Ph.D. in human behavior that will rapidly give you the opportunity to get a handle on the company and the Board, because everything, and I mean everything you do as CEO is about engaging people. So, are you ready?"

"Let's do it," said Bob, sitting down and sipping his coffee.

THE SIX LEVELS OF ENGAGEMENT[5]

"There are six levels at which we can effectively engage people and organizations, Bob. Unfortunately, we've only been trained to focus on the least effective of them – the bottom three, if you will. How would you like to be a master of all six levels of human engagement?"

"That sounds good, sign me up," said Bob.

Jack flipped to a new page and unveiled the Six Levels of Engagement. "These are the six levels at which we can engage people and organizations,"

The Six Levels of Human Engagement
1. Spirit
2. Identity
3. Values & Beliefs
---
4. Capabilities
5. Behaviors
6. Environment

---

[5] The Six Levels of Engagement adapted from work originally developed by NLP Master, Robert Dilts, on Neurological levels of consciousness. NLP includes the study of human behavioral and linguistic patterns. By discovering personal patterns and removing self-induced limits, new levels of awareness and personal effectiveness can be achieved.

said Jack as he listed each of them. "Level 6, The Environment, is at the bottom in terms of effectiveness, and the scale moves upwards to the most powerful, and lasting method of change, Spirit. Let's begin at the bottom," said Jack as he underlined number 6, Environment.

LEVEL 6 – ENVIRONMENT

"Changing the environment focuses on physical change, and typically, as managers, this is where we spend the majority of our time and resources. Yet it is the least effective way to engage people. If you were to compare this model to Abraham Maslow's hierarchy of needs, environment would be the equivalent of satisfying basic survival needs. The environment includes things like safe and comfortable working conditions, adequate tools and technology, salaries and perks like stock options, child care, incentive plans, to name a few. Environmental issues include the carrot and the stick and other measures in an attempt to leverage employee satisfaction and productivity. These things are important because they meet basic needs but, because they are external and not internal motivations, they do little to sway the hearts and minds of people for the long term. And unfortunately, the new 'benefit' soon becomes the expected norm, raising the satisfaction bar even higher.

"Changing these types of environmental factors satisfies in the short term, but does not engage people or make the organization more productive. In fact, after a certain level, continuously improving environmental factors can cost the average organization millions with very little return on investment. I'm not saying don't do these things, Bob, but I want you to be clear why you are doing them, because, by themselves, they rarely influence people to improve productivity on a sustained basis. Unfortunately, all too often, enhancing environmental factors is the primary management tool used to motivate employees."

LEVEL 5 – BEHAVIOR

"As you might imagine, changing individual and organizational behavior can be a real challenge. Most managers try to influence behaviors through fear, while others use praise and reward. This is where behavioral training, such as sexual harassment, diversity training and a company's policies and procedures come in to play. Well, you've probably noticed that training and company policies rarely change employee opinions or values, especially if they believe 'their way' is right or better," Jack remarked. "Trying to legislate morality has always been a losing proposition. From a Judaeo-Christian standpoint, society has gone from ten simple commandments to literally millions of laws, regulations and penalties trying to control people. And while it can be said that they work, at what cost? Every law we pass, every policy we publish says one thing and one thing only: *you are not trusted*. That in itself causes people to do some weird things."

Bob nodded in agreement.

LEVEL 4 – CAPABILITIES

"A little more effective in creating change is adding to or changing people's capabilities," said Jack as he added to the chart.

"We can add to employee capability through training, job sharing, coaching, mentoring or providing new and challenging assignments. These strategies typically take time, money and effort which are not always made available in today's frantic organizations. As an alternative, many companies attempt to improve performance and productivity by hiring 'new and better' performers while terminating the bottom ten percent on an annual basis. This often has the opposite effect from what is intended. Far from motivating people to operate at a higher level, it destroys morale and loyalty to the company. Some organizations are actually training their people to be free agents, further eroding loyalty and forcing many who are not built that way to live in abject fear.

"What do you mean built that way?" asked Bob.

"Success or failure in a role depends largely on personality type.

Great salespeople, for example, are usually dominant, social, driven and independent. They hate structure and would rather be lone rangers. The 'craftsmen', people who are involved in actually making what we sell, however, are less dominant, more analytical, are more patient, detail oriented and cooperative. They love structure, want rules to follow, and need to belong to a team. Trying to make them into free agents is a tremendous waste of energy and does them an awful disservice."

"I see what you mean," said Bob.

"And, for those enlightened companies that can afford to spend millions training their people, here's some bad news. Many in the training business have admitted that up to 80% of all training may be wasted.

"In some cases employees may feel they're being trained because they're in some way not good enough. Often people resent the time away from the job because their work continues to pile up while they are away, and when they get back, they know nothing will have changed and the training will be quickly forgotten in the chaos of the day-to-day."

Bob began to shake his head from side to side, and said, "That seems to be what happened with our Quality Program. All the employees were trained in continuous improvement technique but few of the managers embraced it. No one had the time. Subsequently, important team and project meetings needed to forward the program were not scheduled. Basically, after the consultants left, the program died. We had a good mix of project champions, but even they got tired when people stopped showing up. In this case, the people who didn't show up were the managers. And I must admit, I didn't value the program at the time, either. In the end, the training was lost or only half-heartedly implemented, causing even more frustration and, in some cases, despair."

Jack interjected, "Please don't misunderstand, Bob. Training is absolutely necessary and useful when it is strategically and consciously integrated into an organizational Vision and not just used as a band aid to fix a problem or employee."

"Although these first three change methodologies are not

always as effective as we would like," continued Jack, "they still have an important part to play in the overall change process. If environmental issues, policy and process and *training and development* are not appropriately addressed, the organization will run amuck whether it is standing still or trying to change. And I want to stress the training and development part here.

"So, let's examine what we call the first of the 'transformative' categories. It's much more powerful to inspire change by changing beliefs, or to be more specific, changing limiting beliefs."

LEVEL 3 – BELIEFS

"The truth about beliefs is that *not all beliefs are true!* Yet the world is run by beliefs that are rarely questioned. There's a good reason for this, by the way. Questioning beliefs can cause a lot of unwanted emotion. Look around the world. The biggest reason for bloodshed is individual beliefs. Beliefs are so tied to people's emotions that questioning them can, quite literally, get you killed." Jack pulled the chart he had the day before on the power of beliefs.

"Our Beliefs guide our Emotions, which fuel the kind of Actions we take, or not, that lead to the kind of Results we experience. Positive, affirming beliefs lead to positive affirming emotions, which lead to positive affirming actions. The converse leads more often than not, surprisingly, to inaction."

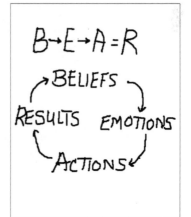

"Hold on, Jack," said Bob, putting his hand out as though to stop him. "I have always prided myself on trying to take the emotion out of my actions and decisions. I'm a very rational person, especially when it comes to work. Now you're telling me that all along my emotions rule? I'm not sure I can buy that."

"This is about as close to a natural law as you can get, Bob. You cannot be without emotion. Let me demonstrate. All day yesterday you challenged and resisted much of what I presented. Not a bad thing, certainly, especially since I invited you to. But let's look at that. Because you 'believed' that much of what I said was 'mumbo-jumbo' or too 'touchy-feely,' your behavior was to discount and resist the process. However, when you were willing to set aside that belief, or at least suspend it for a moment, then the possibility existed that you could change your mind, or belief. Once you changed your belief about the process being 'mumbo jumbo' you were open, tried the activities and experienced a positive result. You didn't go directly from belief to actions, Bob, you went through your feelings."

"So," Bob said pointing to Jack's drawing, "it's a closed loop system – from belief to results?"

"Exactly," agreed Jack, "If we can recognize and change an underlying belief, either in ourselves or others, we will, more times than not, also change the associated feelings and therefore behaviors. And if we can change the behavior, performance will ultimately change. This is an important topic precisely because it is the beginning point for engaging people in a new dialog about the company. We will be talking a great deal about managing corporate beliefs in a few minutes. But as you can see, I have two additional levels that are even more powerful for us to consider. May I continue?"

"Please, do." said Bob.

LEVEL 2 – IDENTITY

Jack underlined the word *Identity* in the number two spot and explained, "The second highest level of human change and engagement is identity. When people are clear about who they are, like you are now, when they are clear about their contribution and values, and claim their true identity, they become more open to questioning and changing their own limiting beliefs and behaviors. They begin to notice when they are out of alignment with their own Core Values, Purpose and Passion, because it affects them emotionally and causes them stress. Pretty much like the pressure around your heart was a signal that there is something not quite right. Many even believe that sickness can be caused by the stress of being out of alignment with your true self."

"I see what you mean. And I guess that's what's meant by the phrase 'being true to yourself,'" Bob said.

"Yes. Now, there are a number of levels of identity. We identify with being American, for example, or being a Marine. You or I see a flag and we're compelled to salute. We also identify with race, family, religion to name a few. There are some important implications here. If you're a good leader, with a clear Purpose and Passion, your people will identify powerfully with your cause. If the cause touches people's values or beliefs or aligns with the Purpose and Passion of your employees, well, you've just tapped into unlimited power for the company. That's related to our third secret, by the way: *Creating a game worth playing.*"

"This is good stuff," said Bob. "So, what you are saying is there are inside and outside identities, and each is a powerful agent to engage people. The most used are the outside identities, yet the most powerful is the inside one," said Bob.

"It is. So, are you ready for the most powerful way to engage people?" asked Jack.

"Absolutely!" replied Bob.

LEVEL 1 – SPIRIT

Jack highlighted the word Spirit in the number one spot on the chart and continued. "Webster's defines Spirit as '*the animating principle of life, especially of humans.*' All of us have our own unique take on Spirit, depending on our cultural or religious background. To me, Spirit is not only a dimension of God, but it is that intangible, universally sublime essence that all human beings share. It's that quality that allows for inspiration to occur, for one's courage to be tapped in service to others, for one's words or deeds to touch another's soul. Spirit is the reason we are here; it's the one thing we have to contribute, the thing joy is made of.

"Tap into the Spirit of your people at Corporate Insights, Bob, and everything below – their Identity, Beliefs, Capabilities, Behaviors and Environment – will come into alignment."

"That's Spirit with a big 'S'," said Jack. "Then there's 'spirit' with a small 's', like team spirit, which Webster calls *'a vigorous sense of group membership.'* Team spirit occurs as a result of capturing the hearts and minds of a group, and uniting them under a common goal thought by them to be meaningful. That's what will develop when you're being 'authentically you', and you bring them into alignment with a compelling Corporate Vision. That's what will occur when your people can believe in something bigger than themselves, and begin working toward something they feel is worthy of their effort, *worthy of giving their life for."* Jack emphasized.

"Have you ever experienced a team with spirit, Bob?"

"Yes. I've had the honor," he said.

"Your military experience?"

"Yes."

"And how would you characterize that experience?" Jack prompted.

"Effortless," Bob said. "Heck, we all seemed to know what to do and showed up just in time to get it done. Like a football receiver, running out for a pass and never looking back, just putting his hands up in the air because he just knew the ball would be there, and it was. We had faith in each other. It was really amazing."

Jack added two words to the chart and said, "What makes this work unique is that we work at the levels of Spirit, Identity and Belief. These are the transformative levels of change."

Bob studied the completed chart.

"Because I've had the chance to work with you, as well as the time to let all this material sink in, I can see that this is an important chart, Jack, and it holds powerful implications for business in general. If all my VPs did was to learn how to focus on the top three, I can't imagine how powerful and effective we could ultimately be. But, I'm having

Six Levels of Human Engagement	
1. Spirit	
2. Identity	*Transformative*
3. Beliefs	
4. Capabilities	
5. Behaviors	*Directive*
6. Environment	

a hard time imagining how I can possibly bring them to a similar place of understanding."

"You probably can't at this point, Bob. Remember, you're still Joe's Kid in their eyes. But there is a powerful process that will get you there. It's called CEOing, and is another tool for the enlightened CEO whose focus   is   on   Creating Extraordinary Organizations.

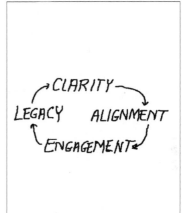

"There are four steps to CEOing that the CEO must *consciously* create:

- Clarity
- Alignment
- Engagement
- Legacy

"CEOing is the overall program we are suggesting to help you do that.   As you will find, there are many levels of CEOing including personal, departmental and organizational.   As we've already experienced, creating Clarity is about broadening your personal awareness. It's the same for departments and entire organizations; the organization as a whole needs to broaden its awareness to understand what drives it and what stops it. The more aware the organization is of its situation, the more powerful it becomes. Awareness includes understanding who we are, where we are, what we believe, our values and where we are going, among other things. That's a lot of territory. Your job as leader will be to help create Clarity for the organization, because until people have choice, they cannot choose to be aligned with where you want to go. And of course, we've already defined what we mean by the term Engagement," said Jack.

"To be challenged, appreciated, responsible and part of something meaningful," said Bob.

"Exactly," said Jack. "So let's continue with exploring how limiting beliefs affect Clarity."

THE TRUTH ABOUT BELIEFS

"As I mentioned a few minutes ago, *the truth about beliefs is that not all beliefs are true.* Yet we tend to operate as if they were. We're born into a world of existing beliefs that cover every aspect our lives. And we generally accept them as truth and take them on as our own. Add to these inherited beliefs, the physical, emotional and psychological trauma that many of us experience in our young lives, and the fact that we automatically install defense systems that run in the background without our conscious knowledge and awareness. And even if we are aware of our beliefs, we say of ourselves, *'being cautious and not trusting is just the way I am.'* But nothing could be further from the truth. This fallacy is also mirrored in organizations when we say, *'that's just the way it is around here.'*"

LIMITING BELIEFS

"Last night I asked you to create a list of limiting beliefs that you believe the organization may be operating under. What did you discover?"

Bob reached for his brief case, opened it and removed a note pad.

"After our timeline work yesterday and uncovering *'cautious'* and *'not trusting'*, I profoundly got the point about limiting beliefs," said Bob. "The biggest limiting belief within our executive team seems to be that *the firefighting we are experiencing is normal.* I understand how they could believe this is normal, because that's what I used to believe myself. I thought reacting rather than planning just came with the territory. The homework you gave me – to list CI's limiting beliefs – has really helped me see that we are not a healthy organization. There's no time to recoup, to think or plan if we're fighting fires," Bob said, "and as CEO, it's up to me to shift the organization away from this unproductive and unhealthy paradigm."

"Good. Is there anything else?" Jack asked.

"This list is a little longer than I thought it would be when I first sat down with it early this morning, but my sense is this is just the tip of the iceberg," said Bob, as he handed the list to Jack.

Jack scanned Bob's list of CI Limiting Beliefs and copied them on a flip chart page.

"Good work," said Jack, "this gives us a lot to start with. Just as we discussed yesterday on the personal level, the major barriers to success in organizations are the invisible ideas, attitudes and

---

Bob's List of Corporate Limiting Beliefs

- Firefighting is accepted as normal in our company
- The acquisition was a mistake
- We can't depend on product quality
- Our development group is not competent
- The management team doesn't like each other
- If you don't come from Oracle or the Big 5 you won't be successful
- There are sacred cows here so we have to walk on egg shells
- The company takes priority over family
- It's not how effective you are, it's how many hours you put in that count
- If I speak up I might set off a land mine

---

beliefs that are held individually and collectively by the organization.

"The first step to neutralizing them on the organizational level, just as on the personal level, is to create the awareness that they even exist. You began the awareness process by generating this list," said Jack, handing the list back to Bob.

"Believe it or not," Jack continued, "simply becoming aware of these will take care of many of them. The process we use will help your organization let go of the stubborn ones as well."

"God, Jack, you're not talking about putting the entire organization in a timeline like we did yesterday, are you? I don't know if I would feel comfortable with that. Can you imagine all that crying?"

They both laughed at the idea.

"No, Bob, we won't be taking your people on a timeline walk into their childhood unless, that is, they request it. Fortunately there are some easier ways to help groups of people let go of limiting organizational beliefs. They are much less threatening to the individual Ego because they are attributed to the organization.

"We want to do two things at this stage. The first is to bring attention to the concept of limiting beliefs, and second, to uncover those that run the organization. By implication, we also raise the issue of individual limiting beliefs.

"So your first job as the new leader is to create clarity for people. Limiting beliefs cloud that clarity. Managing personal and organizational clarity means uncovering the limiting beliefs that hold you back and then having the ability to neutralize them. The most tenacious limiting beliefs, just like this one," said Jack, pointing to Bob's list, *'it comes with the territory'*, "can be especially insidious because it's invisible – people think *'that's just the way it is,'* and don't question it.

"Limiting beliefs are totally invisible to those who share them and silently undermine the creativity and power of an organization. We literally shrink the number of options available to us at any given moment because, in the paradigm of our limited beliefs, these options don't even exist! We can't see or even imagine them. Limiting beliefs leave us operating at a fraction of our potential.

"The easiest, most effective way to improve performance," Jack continued, "is to replace limiting beliefs with empowering ones and give ourselves our options back."

"I can see that, Jack. I'm anxious to address CI's limiting beliefs. What's the plan for doing this?"

"Let's start right now by taking the last one on your list, for example: *'If I speak up, I might set off a land mine.'*"

Jack paused and look at Bob inquisitively, "What imagery do you associate with stepping on a land mine?"

Bob shuddered. "I saw it happen once, in Iraq. Sergeant Frank Harvey was on point about 20 yards ahead of me on this road. He blew up right in front of my eyes. It was horrible. The blast knocked me down and I was covered in his blood. I had nightmares for years after."

Jack nodded sympathetically, "I understand."

"With time, I've been able to put it mostly behind me," Bob said. "But obviously I still associate a lot of pain and terror with the idea of land mines."

"And have you ever verbally stepped on a land mine in the company?" asked Jack.

"Not really," said Bob, "I've been lucky – or have I been cautious?" he wondered. "But I've seen it happen when – Oh-my-gosh!" He sat back in his chair. "That's amazing. I didn't let it happen to me, but I've watched it happen to others. It's the same experience, isn't it? Only now they're mental land mines, not physical ones. I never looked at it that way. It's only because I've been cautious that I've kept myself safe from some of the big blow-ups that have occurred in the company."

"And how did you do that, Bob?" asked Jack.

Bob thought a moment and then he shared, "By not participating fully, by holding back and by not risking myself."

"Excellent. What are the implications to the organization of your belief that you can't trust and that you must be cautious?"

"Well, like me," mused Bob, "I suppose people are going to be overly cautious and reluctant to offer solutions or question what's going on in the organization, especially in a group situation. Or, just like Jim, people become defensive – like I did at the Board meeting on Thursday."

"Can you give me an example of how this plays out among your VPs?" asked Jack.

Bob took a moment to think about Jim's comments and his own recent experiences in staff meetings.

"Meetings have never been a bright spot, but over the year I've been gone meetings have shifted from lackluster to confrontational. And both are unproductive," Bob responded.

"So," said Jack, writing on the chart, "What do we end up with?" asked Jack, pointing to the Board."

Belief	If I speak up I'll step on a land mine
Emotion	Fear, uncertainty, doubt
Action	Fight or Flight
Result	Confrontational or Lackluster meetings

"It looks like a self-fulfilling prophecy," Bob said shaking his head, "we end up getting exactly what we believe."

"Exactly," said Jack, "but if we can change the belief, we will automatically change the result. Because we're all programmed this way, it's a built in success model – if we change our thinking from limiting to empowering beliefs. Garbage in, garbage out, or, good stuff in, good stuff out. You get to pick. As a leader Bob, which one do you want?"

"I'll take what's behind door number two," responded Bob with a wry grin.

"So if you were to transform that limiting belief into an empowering one, what would it be?" asked Jack.

"Speaking up is safe and differing ideas are encouraged and explored with respect," said Bob. "That would certainly change the tenor of our meetings."

For a moment both men were silent.

"So, I'm convinced that we need to overcome our Limiting Beliefs," said Bob. "But I don't have years, I have, what did you say, five quarters?"

"That's why I'm here, Bob," reassured Jack.

"The key to creating rapid transformation is in understanding the dynamics of the Six Levels of Change and focusing on Beliefs, then Identity in a way that allows organizational Spirit to occur. You don't have the years it will take using ordinary behavioral change to have your meetings, or to have anything else at the company, operate effectively. Our understanding of Beliefs, Identity and Spirit allows us to create critical mass and quickly change to the behavior you want from your people. And because everyone experiences the change at the same time, it becomes a lasting change."

"So, Bob, are you ready to articulate exactly what you want?"

"You bet," he emphatically replied.

"FROM-TO" CHARTS

Jack smiled and said, "Good deal! Now, if you were to choose one word or phrase to describe the organization as you experience it today, what would it be?

"Chaos and Uncertainty," said Bob.

"And if you were to choose one word or phrase to describe the organization as you want it to be in 3 to 6 months, what would it be?"

"Clarity and Confidence," said Bob

"So here's what we're going to do," Jack said, "I'm going to step through a number of strategic business areas. Some will be of immediate interest, others you will elect to ignore. I only want you to focus on those areas that will make the biggest difference to the organization right now that you would like completed in 6 months – the mission critical stuff. For this exercise I want you to participate like: 1.*You cannot fail* and 2.*The organization has no limits*. Is that clear?"

How it is now? **Chaos and Uncertainty**	What do I want in 6 months? **Clarity and Confidence**	**Leverage Factor**
Senior staff distrusts each other and it shows in the dysfunctional nature of their interaction and the lack of cooperation between their managers and departments.	As Senior Staff we know each other intimately. We respect and work together to support each other's initiatives. There is seamless cooperation between our departments and us. We are not afraid to remind each other when we act outside of our Passion and Purpose. We walk our talk and are role models for our management team and employees.	
Managers and Supervisors are good technicians with little management training or experience. There is little consistency in process or performance between departments. Little pro-active planning, cooperation or coordination.	Managers and Supervisors are trained to challenge, appreciate and stretch themselves and their people. They are coaches and support the goals and objectives of the organization by insuring their people are fully engaged in growing the company and each other. They measure key success factors.	
The sales force, which is largely made up of former PDQ people, doesn't believe in the product and are suspicious of management's ability to fix it. This lack of confidence shows in their lack of	The sales force is aligned and selling the full potential of our software to new and existing clients with a 6 month sales pipeline	

sales. The pipeline is empty.		
The development effort is stalled because of a lack of ability to align with marketing or stop the fire drills caused by previous bugs. This situation is draining 40% of development engineering resources.	The development effort is in alignment with sales and marketing demand	
Each department is working hard to keep their head above water and is spending no time at all looking at root cause. Blaming others is the pastime.	Departments cooperate and work together with the overall outcome in mind	
Service is unable to keep up with all of the fires and requires up to 40% of development engineering to focus on problem solving in the field.	Service is able to handle customer requests with minimal engineering input	
A them and us attitude exists between the former PDQ development team and the rest of the company	PDQ is fully integrated within CI. There is only CI in the conversation. Development is referred to as Development.	
Existing customer sales are stalled	Existing customer sales are robust	

"Fine," agreed Bob.

As they went through the day, Bob focused on what he really wanted for the organization. Jack captured Bob's desires in the middle of the page.

When Bob completed what he and the Board wanted, Jack had Bob go back and describe how he perceived the current situation to be. Jack captured Bob's thoughts on the left hand side of the page. It wasn't a pretty picture, but Bob persevered and with each admission Bob realized the enormous distance between what he wanted for the organization and where it was today.

"The more I look at this, Jack, the more skeptical I am that we are going to be able to close this gap as quickly as you say we can," said Bob.

WHAT GAP?

"We're not going to be closing any gaps," said Jack. We are going to begin anew. The past is the past and there is nothing anyone can do about it. So as a group, we will appreciate what has worked and simply let go of what didn't. Letting go is a powerful life strategy, Bob – amazing, actually.

"Remember, as we recognize our true selves and change our personal and organizational limiting beliefs we will automatically begin to change the emotions, actions and results attached to them," Jack said as he pointed to the Beliefs flip chart page. "Remember the BEAR formula?"

Bob nodded that he did.

"The old way focused CI's energy on what was wrong, and hunting down the guilty parties to punish. Transforming the organization as an entire group eliminates the need or desire to engage in the politics of 'shame and blame'. In this process we will focus our energy on what we all want and, as a result, become the change we all want to see. Positive peer pressure works wonders. I can't overstate the importance of creating critical mass through a hard reset. It sets the stage for sustainable change."

PEOPLE: THE MOST EFFECTIVE LEVERAGE

As they looked at the chart, Jack asked Bob to mark each line item with either $, T or P, depending on where he saw the most leverage. $ = Money, T = Technology and P = People & Process.

How it is now? **Chaos and Uncertainty**	What do I want in 6 months? **Clarity and Confidence**	Leverage Factor
Senior staff distrusts each other and it shows in the dysfunctional nature of their interaction and the lack of cooperation between their managers and departments.	As Senior Staff we know each other intimately. We respect and work together to support each other's initiatives. There is seamless cooperation between our departments and us. We are not afraid to remind each other when we act outside of our Passion and Purpose. We walk our talk and are	P

	role models for our management team and employees.	
Managers and Supervisors are good technicians with little management training or experience. There is little consistency in process or performance between departments. Little pro-active planning, cooperation or coordination.	Managers and Supervisors are trained to challenge, appreciate and stretch themselves and their people. They are coaches and support the goals and objectives of the organization by insuring their people are fully engaged in growing the company and each other. They measure key success factors.	P
The sales force, which is largely made up of former PDQ people, doesn't believe in the product and are suspicious of management's ability to fix it. This lack of confidence shows in their lack of sales. The pipeline is empty.	The sales force is aligned and selling the full potential of our software to new and existing clients with a 6 month sales pipeline	P
The development effort is stalled because of a lack of ability to align with marketing or stop the fire drills caused by previous bugs. This situation is draining 40% of development engineering resources.	The development effort is in alignment with sales and marketing demand	P
Each department is working hard to keep their head above water and is spending no time at all looking at root cause. Blaming others is the pastime.	Departments cooperate and work together with the overall outcome in mind	P
Service is unable to keep up with all of the fires and requires up to 40% of development engineering to focus on problem solving in the field.	Service is able to handle customer requests with minimal engineering input	P
A them and us attitude exists between the former PDQ development team and the rest of the company	PDQ is fully integrated within CI. There is only CI in the conversation. Development is Development.	P
Existing customer sales are stalled	Existing customer sales are robust	P

"Interesting way to look at things, Jack," said Bob.

"So what do you notice?" asked Jack.

"Virtually all of my issues depend upon leveraging either people or process, more than either technology or money," Bob responded.

"Excellent. You're what we call CEOing."

"CEOing?" asked Bob.

"You remember this?" asked Jack as he brought one of the earlier sheets forward."

"Yes, that was the four step process you said would help bring my VP's up to speed faster."

"Correct," said Jack. "We call the process CEOing, or the process of *Creating Extraordinary Organizations.*" With that Jack added CEOing to the chart. So far we have been focusing on Clarity. It's the awareness of your present circumstance across all four levels of being: Physical, Mental, Emotional and Spiritual, coupled with someplace to go. But we'll come back to all this later."

"No, I think you'd better address that now," insisted Bob.

"Okay." Jack drew four quadrants.

THE FOUR DIMENSIONS OF BEING

"As human beings our physical results are simply a printout of our mental, emotional and spiritual well being. It should be taken as a fact, *that the soft creates the hard.* In every case, negative results are generally connected to inaction caused by negative beliefs or feelings. Very much like

Mental	Physical
What we think, believe and say, either positively or negatively about ourselves and others	What we have or do not have in our lives
Emotional	**Spiritual**
How we feel either positively or negatively about ourselves, others or various situations we find ourselves in	We are either connected or not connected

the BEAR formula we covered earlier. Does this make sense, Bob?"

"Absolutely."

"Good, because there is a reason I'm spending so much time on this."

BUSINESS = P+P MAKING S FOR P

"Business is about people, working with other people, to make 'stuff' for, or to 'serve' people. Because three quarters of this business equation is people-related, it should be no surprise that the majority of our issues are people-related. People offer the biggest leverage to success. Unfortunately, we tend to focus on the 'stuff' or the 'service.' In fact it's downright amazing how much innovation has been invented to eliminate people from the equation simply because we don't know how to harness their potential. I can't tell you how many times I've heard CEOs say 'Things would be great if it wasn't for these damn people.' I once had a CEO hire me and then, when I explained that I needed him for two days, he said, 'Just go fix those people.'"

Bob laughed, and then asked, "So what did you say to him then?"

"I told him sure, but I need to spend two days with you so I'm absolutely sure that I fix them just the way you want me to."

They both laughed at that.

"We can no longer deny that fully engaging people is a key success strategy. You've already experienced the fruits of following this strategy on the battlefield, Bob. You already know what it feels like."

"I don't know what you mean."

"Well," said Jack, who walked over to the sheets still hanging on the wall from yesterday and found the one that was marked *Peak Experience*. He then underlined a few sentences:

"*I was in this slow motion time warp where everything was clear and there was no fear. I pointed and my men went there. I spoke and it happened.*"

"This is what CEOing looks and feels like, Bob," said Jack, pointing to the chart. "Everything works, and the end result is what you intend: winning the battle. Can you see that?"

"I'm not sure; it was all such a blur."

Jack pointed to the CEOing sheet. "How about clear, aligned, engaged troops committed to saving the world?"

"I don't know about saving the world," said Bob as he sat back, thoughtful. After a moment he said slowly, "You might be right. We were clear, aligned and definitely engaged. We were in it together. And I think at some level," pointing to Legacy, "all soldiers must feel they are doing something worthwhile for a cause they believe in, even if that cause is simply to protect the guy next to you. So yes, we knew what to do individually and as a team, we knew why we were doing it, and we had the tools to do it. We definitely had spirit."

"In fact you were so *confident* the enemy could actually see and feel the power of your collective confidence and their hands went up. You won partly because your people on the battlefield were so confident.

"So Bob, let's look at your Purpose again." directed Jack.

"Success depends at least as much on confidence and self esteem as it does on systems, processes or ammunition. In your case your soldiers had been well trained and your relationship with them was strong. Hence, you pointed and the world changed."

> **Confidence & Self Esteem**
>
> With clarity of focus and relentless caring, I inspire myself and others to rise above the chaos, have faith in one another, and risk taking the kind of action the makes a difference in the world.

"That is what happened," affirmed Bob.

"To create CI as a powerful company, we must leverage the people. Would you agree, Bob?"

"Yeah," said Bob, "that's become more and more apparent to me since you walked me through the "From-To" charts. It's clear that the majority of my issues are centered around people and their relationships with each other, which directly impacts performance."

"The key to CEOing, Bob, is to create critical mass by having every member of the organization *experience* first hand the three leadership principles we've been working with over the past two days.

"They will begin to understand and master themselves more fully. They will begin to understand and appreciate each other. And they will decide that they want to play in a game worth playing. Does that make sense?" asked Jack.

"It does, sure, but why the entire organization?" asked Bob. "It seems like overkill."

"Well, remember when I said that you were Joe's kid to your direct reports, that, to them, you weren't the Savior, but just the sales guy who's been out of the loop for the past year?"

"Yeah," Bob recalled.

Leadership Secrets

1. To be Powerful in your life, you must first understand and master yourself

2. To be Powerful with others, you must first understand humanity and master relationships

3. To be Powerful in the world, you must learn to co-create and master a game worth playing

---

"Well, follow that all the way through the organization. If you are Joe's Kid to the VP's, who are the VPs to their managers?"

"Joe's Kid," Bob said.

"And who are the managers to their supervisors?"

"Joe's Kid."

"Supervisors to the average employee?"

"Joe's Kid," said Bob.

"And you can take that same conversation to the Board and your customers as well. We don't see each other as the possibility we are, but only as our past experience of one another. To succeed, to be able to fully leverage the Purpose and Passion in our people, we must let go of our past judgments about them.

Since we live in an Ego-dominated, reactionary world, each person in the organization has a lot riding on having everyone else stay predictable. We need to totally disrupt the kind of predictability that no longer serves us," Jack counseled.

"So, how do we do that?

"We turn the entire structure upside down," said Jack, smiling.

CONSIDER

- Engaged employees feel challenged, appreciated, responsible for the results they produce and part of a game worth playing.

- You engage others by articulating exactly what you want; articulating an inspiring Vision for the company; and helping them experience an expanded reality.

- There are six levels of engagement.

- Managers focus on *controlling* people by focusing on the bottom three levels of the *environment, behaviors and capabilities*.

- Leaders focus on *transforming* people by focusing on the top three levels of engagement: *beliefs, identity and spirit*.

- The truth about beliefs is that not all beliefs are true.

- Our beliefs guide our emotions which fuel the kind of actions we do or do not take, which lead to the results, or legacy we experience. To change the results, we must first change the associated beliefs.

- Our Identity – who we are – includes our unique set of Core Values, Purpose & Passion. These three make up what is commonly called Character.

- Spirit is what connects us to everyone and everything.

- The key to rapid organizational transformation lies in understanding individual and organizational beliefs, identity and spirit.

- By focusing on what you want, there is no need to play catch-up from what you don't want.

- Business is made up of *people*, working with other *people*, making stuff, for *people*.

- The majority of organizational issues revolve around human relationships – people.

- CEOing is the process of Creating Extraordinary Organizations by creating *Clarity, Alignment and Engagement* among people, resulting in our leaving a *Legacy* we can be proud of.

- Transformation: The experience of deep, significant change, after which your perception of yourself and your map of the world has dramatically shifted.

- In the context of CEOing, transformation means that each participant has experienced the three secrets of leadership: They have articulated and are working on mastering self; they foster a compassionate understanding of humanity and are engaged in mastering relationships; they feel passionate about what they are doing and are fully engaged in playing a game that is meaningful to them.

- A transformed organization is aware of the soft stuff. It knows what it believes, how it feels and how every aspect is connected to another.

CHAPTER 15

SHIFTING THE CONTEXT OF BUSINESS

"It is amazing what you can accomplish
if you do not care who gets the credit."
– Harry S. Truman

Jack drew a pyramid. "There are a lot of good, solid reasons for shifting the corporate structure to support a transformed organization. The most compelling is that the existing structure doesn't engage people. This was powerfully supported by research conducted by The Gallup Organization[6] a few years ago. They interviewed 8,000 managers across 400 companies. Only 26% of those interviewed reported being fully 'engaged' in their roles as managers. 55% reported being 'not engaged' or simply reacting to the day-to-day. And 19% reported being 'actively disengaged'.

"I don't think it's a stretch to conclude that if 74% of our managers are running in place, so are our employees. The current business model is 'directive,' and separates and discourages people at every level. But let's examine why.

> **26% Engaged** – employees work with passion and feel a profound connection to their company. They drive innovation and move the organization forward
>
> **55% NOT engaged** – employees are essentially 'checked out.' They are sleepwalking through their workday, putting time – but not energy or passion – into their work
>
> **19% Actively disengaged** – employees aren't just unhappy at work; they're busy acting out their unhappiness. Every day, these workers undermine what their engaged coworkers accomplish

"In simple terms, our current organizational model is a pyramid, with the CEO on top. In this model, the CEO directs VPs, who direct Managers, who in turn direct Employees, who, in far too many cases, try to direct Customers.

---

6 2003 Gallup Organization Study on employee engagement

"Remember what we said about energy following focus? In the Directive model, the entire organization is focused on growing revenue and profit and pleasing the boss. Yet what people want is to be challenged, appreciated, responsible and part of something meaningful."

"I disagree," countered Bob. "We have ISO standards of operational performance that we follow, and now we even have Sarbanes-Oxley as an ethics standard, and how about serving the customer as a focus?"

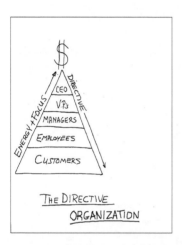

THE DIRECTIVE
ORGANIZATION

"Okay, let me take serving the customer first," replied Jack. "Is serving the customer the actual purpose of the company? Or is it really a strategy employed to achieve the purpose of profit?"

"Hmmm, I see what you mean; Customer service would be a strategy to get to profit," Bob conceded.

"Now let's look at ISO, an outside standard, and Sarbanes-Oxley, another outside standard. By outside standard, we mean a set of performance standards others expect of you. Were either one of these outside standards generated out of 'possibility'. Or 'lack of trust?'" asked Jack.

"I suppose from a lack of trust," said Bob.

"Exactly. And let's look at continuous improvement programs while we're at it. How much success do you think companies have achieved with them, or the latest rage in reengineering?"

"Judging from our recent quality program, not much," admitted Bob.

"And they will continue to miss their full potential as long as these programs spring from a lack of trust in people to do the right thing. Many will disagree, of course, but you just look at the effect these programs have had on performance. Many of these programs are installed and administered by outside organizations rather than the people who will be using them.

"Early quality programs pitted the American worker against the Japanese, and now the Chinese. These programs suggested the American worker was not good enough, and Sarbanes-Oxley blatantly says that our business leaders are not to be trusted. I recently read an article saying that the age of the Imperial CEO is finally over. Believe me; people only give lip service to programs that are put in place to police them.

"It may sound like I'm disparaging these programs, but I'm not. I actually think these programs can be valuable and can add to both productivity and ethics, but to be fully implemented at every level, they need to come from a different place; *they must serve human Purpose and Passion* rather than simply react to and police human behaviors.

"Without Purpose and Passion an organization operates from the 'survival instinct' or, said another way, from its collective 'Ego,'" said Jack. "The underlying belief is that the purpose of an organization is solely to make a profit for shareholders, and *without profit we perish*. This kind of single minded and fear-based thinking pretty much guarantees people will resort to any means to survive. The end begins to justify the means."

"I can see that taking place in more than just business," said Bob, shaking his head.

"Well, let's explore this a little more," said Jack as he added a chart to the right of the directive pyramid, "and see how we can benefit from this understanding."

WORKING 'IN'

"Would you agree that profit is going to rely on a high degree of productivity, and that high productivity is dependent on high employee engagement?"

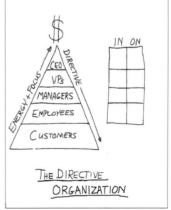

"Yes, I'll give you that," responded Bob. "Notice this IN and ON chart[7]," motioned Jack. "IN is the amount of time you and your people currently spend working IN the organization; developing, making and servicing product, putting out fires, handling issues between departments, focusing on employee issues – pretty much handling the status quo. Agreed?"

"Okay," said Bob.

"And ON is the amount of time you are currently engaged in growing the company – planning, thinking, training, breaking down barriers for your organization, improving and deepening customer relationships. Does that make sense?"

"Okay," Bob agreed, "I'm with you so far."

"Good. On a scale of 1-100, with 1 being 'not much' and 100 being 'a lot', how much time do you think you personally spend working ON versus IN the company? Jack asked.

Bob thought about the question for a few minutes.

"So far, even with all my field visits, I've spent about 90% of my time working IN and only 10% ON. And judging from my recent conversations with Jim, his time was spent about the same," Bob admitted.

"A wake up call for me," Bob silently thought.

"Okay, let's move down the pyramid. How do your VPs, managers and employees spend their time?" Jack pressed on, filling in Bob's answers on the chart as they went.

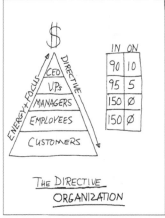

"This isn't going to look too good," Bob sighed, "I'd say my VP's spend 95% IN and maybe, if they're lucky, 5% ON. And, Managers, well, after this trip I just took, I'd say up to 150% IN and 0% ON. The same goes for the average employee."

"Why do you say 150%?" Jack interjected.

---

[7] Michael Gerber's *E-Myth* in-and-on concept applied to the entire organization.

"Because our managers and employees are working 50-60 hour weeks," Bob confessed.

"Why do you think they work so much overtime, Bob?" Jack asked.

"Clearly, because we're stuck in reaction, and spending too much time fighting fires. I guess you would say that we're operating entirely out of our Ego, not out of our Purpose and Passion."

Jack smiled, and then took a minute and updated the new pyramid and chart.

"So does working for the status quo work for you?"

"No, not at all," said Bob.

"Good. So what would happen if we did this?"

WORKING 'ON'

Jack drew an up-side-down pyramid.

"What if we moved from a directive organization to what we call a transformative organization?

"In this model, the Board supports the CEO in *being* a particular way, who supports the VPs in *being* a particular way, and the VPs support the Managers in *being* a particular way, who in turn support the Employees in *being* a particular way, who support the Customer in *being* a particular way. Notice where everyone's focus is now?" Jack directed, pointing to the bright yellow star at the top of the up-side-down pyramid.

"Obviously the focus is on being a particular way. But what way are we all being?" asked Bob, with a tinge of irritation in his voice. "This conversation is headed to woo-woo land again," said the thought in his head. Then he smiled, and said, "Thanks for sharing," to the thought and moved on. He was beginning to notice his Ego's voice in the background more often.

"Whatever way you want them to be, Bob," said Jack. "The

only requirement is that the 'being-ness' must be inspirational to you and your people. But before we get to actually defining what this 'being-ness' might be, I'd like to make a quick detour. What's CI's current Vision statement?"

Bob looked a little blank, then he smiled and said, "I don't recall."

"Just notice that," said Jack. "Okay, what do you think your Vision statement would have been if we hadn't had this little conversation?"

"About being first in the industry, profit and pleasing shareholders," mused Bob.

"Exactly," said Jack. And there is nothing wrong wanting to be number one or with wanting profit and pleasing shareholders. It's just that profit and pleasing shareholders doesn't inspire the soul. It doesn't provide the impetus for an inspiring 'way of being,'" noted Jack.

"Yes. But I have a question," Bob interjected with some impatience. "What about all the hundreds, if not thousands of successful companies out there who are out for profit and who haven't examined their corporate Vision statements for compatibility with the CEO's Purpose and Passion, or who aren't looking for ways to implement some magical *way of being?*"

"Who says they are successful?" replied Jack. "Are they successful because they hit their profit targets by floating inventory all over the country in tractor trailers so they can show product shipped? Or loading up distributors only to take product back in the next quarter? Or hiring fancy accounting firms with tricky

---

Leadership Secrets

1. To be Powerful in your life, you must first understand and master yourself

2. To be Powerful with others, you must first understand humanity and master relationships

3. To be Powerful in the world, you must learn to co-create and master a game worth playing

---

Primary Motivators of Fortune 1000 CEOs	
Fear	43%
Power	22%
Money	7%

accounting practices to defer expenses? All these unethical actions, and much worse, come from a way of being, Bob. It's called fear. In fact, according to a 2004 study[8] of 208 Fortune 1000 CEOs, 43% said Fear was their primary motivation, with 22% noting Power and 7% saying money.

"Now let me ask you, which company do you think will generate more profit, a company that reflects *Clarity & Confidence* operating out of Purpose and Passion, or one that reflects Chaos & Uncertainty operating out of fear?"

"Obviously the one that reflects Clarity and Confidence," said Bob.

"Good, so what do you think your corporate Vision Statement might be if you accept the premise that profit is a more likely result of a Purpose driven organization?

"I'm not yet sure." Bob admitted.

"Are you ready to find out?" asked Jack.

"Yes, of course." replied Bob.

"Remember early on yesterday I told you that there were three key Leadership Secrets?

Bob nodded yes and said, "I remember."

"Well, we've been working on these secrets all along, and I want to keep demonstrating your progress. Number one has everything to do with your Purpose & Passion statement and this 'way of being' we have been discussing. In large part they provide the answers to these questions.

- Who am I?
- What am I capable of?
- Why am I here?

Confidence & Self Esteem

With clarity of focus and relentless caring, I inspire myself and others to rise above the chaos, have faith in one another, and risk taking the kind of action the makes a difference in the world.

"Read your Purpose & Passion statement, aloud, please, Bob"

Bob read aloud from the chart on the wall.

---

[8] Reported in the St. Louis Post-Dispatch, 03/26/2004

Jack turned to Bob and said, "Going back to previous comments about 'being' a certain way – would you say your Purpose statement exemplifies a way of being?"

Bob nodded in agreement.

"And this way of being is, in your words from before, a contribution to humanity?"

Again, Bob nodded yes to the question.

"Then let me ask you, Bob. Is it possible for an organization to have a Vision, a 'way of being' that contributes to humanity, in the same way that you have created this for yourself as an individual?"

Individual Questions	Organizational Questions
- Who am I?	- Who are we?
- What am I capable of?	- What are we capable of?
- Why am I here?	- Why are we here?

"Well, I guess I never thought about it before. At least not like that. I mean, we make software products," Bob reminded Jack with just a bit of sarcasm. "How does making software relate to contributing to mankind?" asked Bob.

"Well, why couldn't the software products CI designs and produces serve humanity?" Jack prodded.

Bob was silent for a few moments. He looked at Jack and said, "Well, they give our clients more control over their projects, more powerful results."

"So your software products can help your customers be more powerful?" Jack repeated.

"And how does this contribute to humanity?" pressed Jack.

Again, Bob paused before replying. He spoke slowly as if thinking out loud, "We design software – software that is supposed to make the enterprise easier to manage. To improve enterprise visibility by helping managers recognize and manage the most important projects with the greatest possibility of return to the organization. And, well, our contribution may be to allow people more time at home with less stress, like that."

"Good," said Jack, "now, as you look at all of this, if there were one perfect overarching statement that would bring your dream to life, a statement that would inspire you and all of your stakeholders in working together to fulfill on these intentions," Jack pointed to the charts, "what would it be?"

Bob stood back from the wall and for several minutes read and re-read the charts. He then sat down in a comfortable chair with a pad of paper and wrote several different concepts on his pad. Finally he said, 'Be Powerful,' I would have us all Be Powerful.

"Excellent," said Jack as he went to the star over the upside down pyramid and wrote *Be Powerful* near the star.

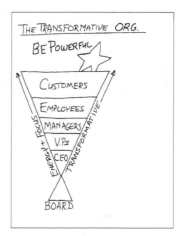

"In the transformative organization you will be able to consciously shift people from only working IN to working some portion of their time ON the organization. Let's take a look at what might work for Corporate Insights."

THE PROCESS OF ENGAGEMENT

"As we saw earlier, the default position of a reactive organization is that few people are engaged in working 'on' the organization. But let's just say that we are successful at transforming CI to a supportive, creative organization, an organization with a clear Purpose and engaged people. Remember, they are now challenged, appreciated, responsible and loving where the organization is going. How do you want to allocate 'in' and 'on' time for the new CI? Let's begin with you. How

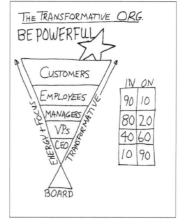

much time do you want to be working 'on' the organization?" asked Jack.

"I would think just the opposite from before. 10 percent IN and 90 percent ON."

"And your VPs?"

"40/60."

"And your managers?"

"80/20."

"Employees?"

"The exact opposite of me, 90/10."

"Excellent work," said Jack, walking over to the wall to pull the directive chart and place it side-by-side with the transformative chart. "So let's see how this compares to a directive/reactive organization."

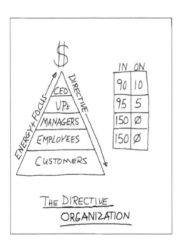 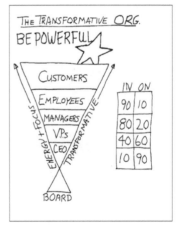

"Wow," said Bob, "this puts a lot more feet on the ground doesn't it?"

"Yes it does."

"So what you're saying, Jack, is by focusing on something truly meaningful to people we can engage them more fully than we have in the past. But how do we get people to actually work *on* their roles, by just assigning them more time?"

"Good question," said Jack. "You don't assign them anything. You don't require. You inspire. Listen, Bob, these are smart people who want to do a good job. We just have to give them a nudge in the right direction. We simply need to transform them."

Jack stood there with a grin on his face.

"And how are we going to do that?"

"Well, first, let's make sure that's what you want. Let's compare the Directive and the Transformative models and see if there is enough benefit before we get into exactly how we will transform them. Let's look at why we should do it."

Jack flipped over a sheet he had prepared earlier and went through each point.

Directive Organization	Transformative Organization
Ego Driven – Reactive	Purpose Driven – Creative
Management Focus is on generating revenue and profit while pleasing the boss	Leadership Focus is on holding the level above you accountable to the Corporate Vision, Mission, Values and Code of Honor
Vision/Mission/Values created by Senior Management and presented to employees	CEO creates Vision. Manager and Employee teams design the Mission, Values and Code of Honor to achieve the Vision
Communication from top down.	Communication up, down and sideways
Mission is often overridden by need to generate profit	Mission is critical to the organization and understood by every member
Process is given, Employees are managed	Process is managed, Employees are led
The organization is unbalanced, working solely 'in' the company maintaining the status quo.	The organization is balanced, working 'in' the organization to deliver product and services to the customer, while at the same time, working 'on' the organization at every level to improve both internal and external customer service
The majority of people are disengaged	The majority of people are fully engaged. (Where engaged means challenged, appreciated, responsible and part of a game worth playing.)
Develops Expert Fire Fighters	Develops Expert Process Designers
High overtime, low productivity	Low overtime, high productivity
Employees Required	Employees Inspired
Burn out	Passion

"The key ingredient here is to shift the organization from performing just the status quo activities to also embrace project driven growth activities.

"So, which do you want CI to be? A directive or transformative organization?"

"Transformative," said Bob.

"Would it make a difference to where CI is today?"

"Absolutely," replied Bob, who paused to think about it further. "We'd have a lot fewer fires and a lot more time to put a dent in my strategic goal list."

"So *Being Powerful* in whatever we do could be the Vision of the company?"

"Is that what you want?" Jack handed the question back to Bob.

"I really like the possibility," said Bob thoughtfully, "but who defines what it is to *Be Powerful?*"

"You and your people do, Bob; using a process that fully engages them. Would you like to know how?"

"Yes, absolutely," said Bob.

CONSIDER

- With all of our MBA's, technology and best practices, only 26% of our managers and employees are engaged in their jobs while 55% are disengaged and 19% are actively disengaged.

- The current business model is directive. It separates and discourages people at every level. It gives up on people and demonstrates this by firing the bottom 10% as a solution to disengaged workers rather than getting to one of the root causes: a lack of inspiring leadership.

- The focus on share-holders and profit, rather than on employee and organizational Purpose and Passion and customer satisfaction, dehumanizes the workplace.

- People, and that means all of us, want to be challenged, appreciated, responsible and part of something meaningful.

- Without Purpose and Passion, an organization operates from its 'survival instinct' or, said another way, from its collective Ego. This kind of fear-based thinking pretty much guarantees people will resort to any means to survive. The end begins to justify the means.

- Fear is the prime motivator of Fortune 1000 executives.

- Sarbanes-Oxley is a reaction to Ego-driven organizations.

- In the current directive model, few people actually work 'on' the organization.

- In the new transformative model, the majority of people also work ON the organization at their level of expertise.

- To engage people, expose them to the three secrets.

CHAPTER 16

ALIGNING & ENGAGING PEOPLE

In the end, we all want the same things.
Few go to work to do a bad job. Do you?

"Remember when I said finding yourself is the easy part, and that the hard part would be being who you were meant to be?" asked Jack.

"Yes, you made that point a few times," replied Bob.

"Well, aligning and engaging people believe it or not, is also pretty easy once you know how," said Jack. "The hard part will be having the courage to be true to yourself and to the Vision of the company once the shift is made."

"I've never experienced any of this being easy, Jack. And I guess I resent the implication that I'm stupid."

"Who's implying that, Bob?" asked Jack, gently.

Bob turned red, "I guess I am, or, at least, my Ego is."

"Good catch. Listen, I run into this a lot. We can transform an organization so fast it can make your head spin. It's like magic. But what is magic?"

"A sufficiently advanced technology that few are yet aware of," said Bob.

"Exactly. So are you ready to learn the secret to rapid organizational transformation so that you can do it yourself in the future?

"Let's get on with it."

"Aligning and engaging an organization looks like this." Jack handed Bob a chart and flipped the page. "We call it the Accelerated Transformation Map. There are two phases with seven steps. Phase One begins with the hard reset. It begins with every person in the organization uncovering his or her Values, Purpose and Passion. The CEO creates a Corporate Vision and Strategic Plan. The VPs consider all the implications of the Vision and

Strategic Plan. The VP's set a Leadership Charter to support the Vision and Strategic Plan. The Managers consider all of the

---

Accelerated Organizational Transformation Map

Phase 1: Hard Reset

1. CEO Transformation and creation of the Corporate Vision and Strategic Plan
2. VP Transformation and Alignment with the Vision and Strategic Plan and the creation of a Leadership Charter
3. Manager Transformation and Alignment with the Vision, Strategic Plan and Leadership Charter and the initial draft of Corporate Values and Code of Honor
4. Employee Transformation and Alignment behind the Vision, Leadership Charter. Further refinement of Values and Code of Honor. Development of the Corporate Mission
5. Specific Projects to re-design corporate structures to be in supportive of the culture's full engagement in the Strategic Plan

Phase 2: Sustaining Engineering

6. On-going 90 Day Progress Ritual to overcome corporate entropy
7. The New Employee Course welcomes new employees into the organization by helping them articulate their own Purpose & Passion statement while introducing them to the unique story of CI's Vision, Mission, Values, Code of Honor and Strategic Plan

---

implications of the Vision, Strategic Plan and the Leadership Charter. They then suggest a set of Values and a Code of Honor[9] to support the Vision and the Leadership Charter. The employees

consider all the implications of the Vision, Leadership Charter, Values and Code of Honor. The employees, in groups of one to two hundred add their perspective to the Values and Code of Honor, and then, each group creates a version of the Corporate Mission. When all employee groups have added their perspective to the Values and Code of Honor, and contributed their version of the

---

[9] As in the Marine Corps, a set of simple, powerful rules that govern the internal behavior of a team, along with the ability of the team itself to enforce these rules. Example: Never leave a man behind.

Corporate Mission, one employee from each employee group will assemble and, using everything that came before, will create a final version of CI's Mission for adoption by the entire organization."

Bob was okay until Jack hit number four, Mission development, when he became upset and exploded, "There is no way that management should ever let employees create the Mission Statement. No way! That would cause all kind of problems. They don't understand what needs to be done, and we should have some control over what they do. We should have veto power. I don't agree with that at all."

Jack, who had been taking notes, just sat back and just smiled. "So where is that coming from Bob?"

Bob just shot Jack a look of disbelief, "What do you mean where is that coming from? Experience, that's where it's coming from. You can't depend on employees to do that level of thinking; they barely know what to do on a good day."

Jack calmly walked over to the flip chart on the wall titled Limiting Beliefs. He took it from the wall and placed it back on the easel and began writing on it.

"So Bob, do you really believe this garbage?" said Jack, pointing to what he had written on the Limiting Belief sheet.

"I didn't say that!"

"Of course you did, because you were operating out of your Ego self. Now the question is, do you really believe what you just said? Because if you do, there is no hope for changing anything at CI."

For the first time since they were together Bob was truly angry. His face was flushed, and he almost shouted at Jack, "Who the hell do you think you are?" but he quickly caught himself and clenched his teeth instead.

But there it was, in black and white, right next to his Purpose and Vision Statement. Bigoted, unjust, unfair accusations leveled

---

Bob's Limiting Beliefs

- Management can't depend on employees to create Mission
- Employee involvement would cause problems
- Employees don't know what to do on a good day
- Employees don't understand what needs to be done

against his employees. He had said those things. Did he really believe them? Or was this just another knee-jerk reaction to a perceived loss of control?

"I can understand your frustration Bob," offered Jack, "it can certainly seem as though people don't want to participate, and it can seem as though they are not capable, even if given the opportunity. Your negative reaction to employee participation at this level is predictable because CI's current operating context is directive. Remember, a directive organization by its very nature discourages collaboration and participation. The directive model creates separation and promotes cynicism, doubt and lack of trust. It encourages the Dilbert myth at every level, where *all bosses are generalized as idiots and all employees as helpless and hopeless.* It's a myth many of us have accepted as true. But it is not true. The good news is that you are not compelled to continue using the directive model."

There was a long period of silence.

"You're a quick study Bob. We discussed more than once that it would be difficult to be true to yourself, so apply what you learned over the last two days. What is behind your anger and lack of trust? Are you coming from fear or from possibility with all this anger?" asked Jack, pointing to the EP Chart on the wall.

"I guess I came from the Ego side – from the fear." said Bob, surprising himself at how quickly he was letting go of his anger.

"Fear of what?" Jack wanted to know.

"I'm afraid of losing control."

"And what does that mean?" prompted Jack.

"I guess I'm afraid that if I lose control that I'll fail like Jim did."

The two sat there for a moment just looking at one another.

"Bob, being willing and able to name your fear and face it is powerful. When you can do this, several things occur. The first thing that happens is that you are able to see the incredible power that fear and its counterpart, anger, have over you. Next, you get to decide if you want to continue to operate from the negative frame of fear and anger. This frame will either serve your Purpose or it will not. And then choose – do I continue with the negative, as I have in the past, or do I make a change?"

CHOOSE AGAIN PROCESS

"This is a process that I call 'choose again.' Just because you've chosen fear/anger/lack of trust, doesn't mean you're stuck with these choices. I know it sounds simplistic, but it *is* possible to simply 'choose again,' to operate from possibility rather than a fear based mode. Sometimes choosing again may take some time, and we may resist. Other times, we can literally 'choose again' in the moment that we realize we are not benefited by our original fear-based choice.

"Take a look again at these beliefs and tell me what you're thinking," concluded Jack.

After looking at the limiting beliefs chart for a moment, Bob said, "I've been concerned with control ever since I learned I was being considered for the CEO slot. Because getting the job was such a surprise I've often felt at a loss, and

> **Bob's Limiting Beliefs**
>
> - Management can't depend on employees to create Mission
> - Employee involvement would cause problems
> - Employees don't know what to do on a good day
> - Employees don't understand what needs to be done

I worry that I'll make some big mistakes. I don't want to fail like Jim did."

"You won't."

"How can you be so sure?"

Jack pointed to the Limiting Beliefs chart and said, "Because, by acknowledging these as limiting beliefs based upon fear, you just let go of the kind of judgmental garbage that keeps most people stuck. You just experienced letting go of your Ego.

"Whenever you are angry, impatient, upset or afraid, check in to see where you are coming from. Is it from fear or from possibility? Is it from your Ego or from your Purpose, your head or your heart, your lower self or your higher self?

"We all have to practice letting go of our limiting beliefs, negative judgments and our fears. That's what's called mastering yourself. Mastery just takes practice. Mastery isn't perfection, Bob, it's simply a commitment to progress. And it will be a lot easier when everyone in your sphere of influence is practicing this as well.

"So summarize for me Bob. What are you thinking and how do you want to go forward?"

"You want me to say 'choose again' don't you, Jack?

"It's not what I want, Bob. What do you want for yourself, your employees, and CI? What's your corporate Vision?"

"Be Powerful," responded Bob.

"What will it take to begin to bring this Vision to CI?" asked Jack.

"I guess I'm going to have to Be Powerful," laughed Bob, "and change my own limiting beliefs – to choose again – to trust that CI's employees will contribute in a meaningful way. And not just to this Mission Statement you were describing, but to trust that they probably want CI to succeed as much as I do.

"Instead of being afraid, I need to remind myself that my Passion is bringing Confidence and Self Esteem to others," Bob concluded.

Jack smiled as Bob spoke and when he was done Jack said, "Congratulations Bob, I'd say your personal transformation has begun."

"Thanks Jack."

"How about a break before we pick up where we left off?"

Bob nodded his agreement, stood up, stretched and walked outside to enjoy the water, the ducks and the sunshine.

When they came back from their break Jack went back to the process of aligning and engaging people. He pointed again to the transformation map, specifically statement #4.

"This Mission piece is a deliberate set up on our part to stop people in their tracks by demonstrating how little belief we have in one another. It's an exercise we created to demonstrate how limiting beliefs destroy the promise of empowerment. Believe me, it creates a lot more upset in large groups, but in every case it gives people a highly visible look at how they are behaving, compared to who they really are. Just like you had some limiting beliefs to let go of about your employees, your employees have more than a few they need to let go about you."

"What do you mean?" asked Bob.

"Well, here are just two employee limiting beliefs that I predict are alive and well in CI," said Jack.

- Management doesn't know what it is doing
- Management doesn't trust us

"The truth of the matter is that management is the group that needs empowerment. So the promise in flipping the organization is that every employee empowers you, believes in you. Imagine what that would feel like!"

"I can't imagine. Especially since I've always understood it's the CEOs job to empower other people. How can the people I'm supposed to be empowering be the ones who empower me?" asked Bob.

EMPOWERMENT

"We define empowerment as *having faith in others such that they begin to have faith in themselves.* The truth is that when your people are transformed, when they begin to let go of the limiting beliefs that hold them back, you will find that they are a lot smarter and have a lot more wisdom than you ever thought possible. And in the Mission exercise we get to demonstrate how smart they are over and over again. Not one company I've ever worked with has changed a word of what the employees have come up with in this exercise. And let's face it: if your employees, of all people, can't articulate the corporate Mission, how far do you think you will get as a company? If they're not the ones to understand and articulate the Mission, who the heck should?

"But that doesn't mean we don't fully prepare them to handle the Mission development task, Bob. Empowerment isn't simple delegation. As leaders, we should know exactly what they will need to accomplish the task – and we make sure they have it. We prepare them to be successful.

"In the Directive organization, management hammers out the Mission and posts it on the wall like another directive. Not a memorable way to engage people in the Mission. It's no different than giving them another set of rules to follow.

"But in the transformative organization everyone participates in the creation of these cultural documents and yes, they also post them on the wall, but now the employees take them very seriously.

"Here's an overall visual of our *organizational model* and all of its soft influences. We filled in the *human model* yesterday during your Visioning session, and have been working on the organizational model all day today."

After pulling up the human model Jack dad drawn the day before, he drew the organizational model for Bob to consider.

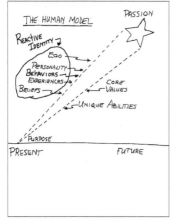 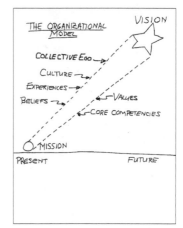

As Jack drew it, Bob saw that it was similar to the human model except for some different terminology. What influenced and guided him in his Purpose and Passion, --like beliefs and experience -- also seemed to influence and guide organizations. Living the corporate Vision would require self discipline from the members. It would have to know itself and act in alignment with its Values, Mission and Vision" in order to remain in organizational integrity.

"So, Bob," asked Jack, "can you be fulfilled leading an organization where the Vision calls employees to *Be Powerful* in everything they do?

"Yes, I think so," said Bob.

"And won't such an organization need a leader who *inspires confidence and self esteem?*"

Bob sat there humbled after his earlier non-trusting comments.

"Yes, and I can do that," said Bob with renewed confidence.

"So let's look at each component of the model. Notice that human passion maps directly to organizational Vision."

The Human Model	The Organizational Model
Passion – describes what a person is living/giving their life for. The contribution they are making to mankind. What brings them joy and gives them energy. The ultimate value one brings to others	**Vision** – describes the possibility of who people can BE and the contribution they can make in fulfilling the Mission. The ultimate value the organization brings to its customers
Purpose – describes what a person brings to the roles they play in life. Who they are simply by being alive. What they DO in life that is in alignment with and supports their Passion	**Mission** – describes what people are expected to DO in order to fulfill the possibility of the Organizational Vision
Values –describes the attributes a person is born with that serve to guide their words, thoughts and actions. Along with Passion & Purpose, an element of one's Character	**Values** – describes how people are expected to behave in order to achieve the organizational Mission and Vision
Unique Abilities – describes the natural, God given talents that support a person's authentic Passion and Purpose	**Core Competencies** – describes the skills, talents and abilities necessary to support the organizational Mission and Strategies
Beliefs – Gateways to action or inaction by controlling human emotions. Adopted and developed by the Ego as a consequence of birth and experiencing life. Not necessarily true. Beliefs can either support or limit the full expression of one's Purpose and Passion	**Beliefs** – Gateways to action or inaction by controlling organizational morale. Adopted and developed by the collective Ego as a reflection of founder and member collective beliefs and work experiences. Not necessarily true. Beliefs can either support or limit the full expression of an organization's Mission and Vision
Personality – Describes a series of preferences or tendencies within an individual to act a particular way. The degree of Dominance over Acceptance; Sociability over Analytical; Patience over Drive; and Compliance over Independence	**Culture** – Describes a series of preferences or tendencies within an organization to act a particular way. The degree of Dominance over Acceptance; Sociability over Analytical; Patience over Drive; and Compliance over Independence
Ego – The automatic tendency of the individual to react to any perceived threat to the body or psyche	**Collective Ego** – The automatic tendency of the organization to react to any perceived threat to the status quo

"Excellent. So let's review the human and corporate models more closely and then, and if it's okay with you, we will take a look at exactly what can keep you and your organization from achieving your intention.

"So you already know what will get in the way?" asked Bob.

"Of course," said Jack while laughing heartily.

ENSURING SUSTAINABILITY

"Quickly moving people to another level of performance is not so difficult, Bob, but keeping them growing is another matter. Organizations, just like people, have what we call a *collective ego*, and are wired to survive – to keep things just as they are by clinging to the status-quo. The problem is, the collective ego works to keep things just as they are *even if things aren't very good*. It resists ALL change.

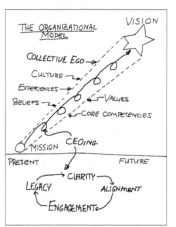

"In addition to the effects of the collective ego, we were also faced with what we call *human entropy*. Human entropy is the tendency of people in motion to slow down and forget why they were in motion to begin with."

"How long before people really begin to slow down?" asked Bob.

"Good question, we really had to work on that, but the short story is 90 days. If you don't reinforce strategy, for example, every 90-days, kiss it good by."

"Interesting," commented Bob.

"It really is," said Jack, "and so we needed to build in a 90-day self-correcting device to overcome these organizational traits if we were going to be successful at sustaining the transformative organization. It needed to contain all of the elements of CEOing," said Jack, pointing to the Organizational Model, "and so we simply called it *The CEOing ritual.*"

"Ritual?"

"Yes," said Jack. "A ritual provides the mechanism to build

habit into the organizational DNA. Sustainability depends on it.

"Running the CEOing ritual every 90-days mitigates the effects of the collective ego and human entropy by regularly engaging every person at every level in the organization. This insures people continue to feel challenged, appreciated, responsible and part of something that is still meaningful. In short, we don't give people the time to forget who they really are."

LOGISTICS

"Hell of a model, Jack."

"Thank you."

"So let's talk about the logistics of this process. I really appreciate the transformational approach, but I'm not sure if we can afford..."

"The time and money?" interjected Jack.

"I guess I've got that particular limiting belief down really well!" said Bob, laughing.

"How many people do you have, Bob?"

"I don't know exactly, I think 400 or so."

"Just..."

"I know, I know, just notice that!" said Bob

"Good catch, Bob," said Jack. "And, what if there was a way to do what we've done together, plus a whole lot more, with hundreds of people at the same time. Would time still be that big of a factor?"

"Well, I imagine it would still be a challenge to pull that many people together. But no, it would be doable."

"And if we were able to facilitate hundreds of people at the same time the cost would be more manageable as well, don't you think?"

"I would hope so. I mean I can't afford ten grand for every person in the company. But something tells me you already know that."

Jack smiled. "You're right. We've been down this path before. I can assure you, every CEO has said going through the process was well worth the money. We've experienced ROIs in the 5x -10x range in the first 12 months."

"We'll see," said Bob.

"Well, looking at your intentions for the two days, you can boil them down into three mandates.

"First, rapidly transform the company.

Intentions

1. Integrate PDQ quickly into the rest of the company
2. Get our leadership leading instead of fighting
3. Reduce expenses and improve throughput and sales revenue
4. Learn more about myself and my leadership style
5. Learn to be an effective CEO faster than I would on my own
6. Quickly tie what I learn here into results for the organization
7. Discover some useful things about my people I'm not seeing yet

---

"Second, bring everyone, including the PDQ guys, quickly into alignment with your Vision.

"And third, fully engage all employees at every level in achieving your key strategic initiatives," said Jack while counting them off on his fingers.

"And you guarantee PDQ gets integrated," added Bob.

"If we do the process I've outlined, the integration is guaranteed," said Jack. "However, you're going to have to be willing to risk some fallout. Sometimes, once you've shared a clear Vision of the future and the team creates its new ground rules, there may be some people who decide they just aren't willing to play the new game."

"What do you mean exactly?" asked Bob.

"Some may simply realize that they've been unhappy doing the job for some time and the process will help them see how conflicted they've been. This can be a very positive outcome for the individual and for CI. Others may feel uncomfortable with their newly uncovered Purpose or the organization's new Vision and simply choose not to participate. And then, of course, it will be up to you to let some people go based upon your own observations of their willingness or ability to work within the new paradigm."

"I understand," said Bob thoughtfully. "But holding on to people who should move on is not good for the morale of the troops. I've seen it before. In fact, I've often thought Jim was a bit slow to let people go. At the time it seemed like it was the lesser of two evils to keep them."

"That's often the case, Bob," said Jack. "But keep in mind, too, that some people might surprise you and come around. I've seen people who were on the edge of the bubble – and through this process they were able to find new passion and vitality and totally let go of non-transformative beliefs and behaviors."

"And what happens if this process doesn't deliver?" asked Bob.

"Then of course, you don't pay us."

Bob looked at Jack with surprise, "How can you afford to take that kind of a risk?"

"When I deal with Ego alone, life can be pretty unpredictable. But when I deal with an individual's Purpose & Passion, I have the honor of dealing with pure desire and integrity. I don't consider it a risk.

"But that doesn't mean we won't run into some resistance," added Jack. "Like I said, it's not unusual for a few VPs or managers to fall out once the process is completed."

"Fair enough," said Bob, "I do have some reservations about a few people even being willing to participate, but let's start the process. I'll have Rebecca begin scheduling each of my direct reports to go through the two day Visioning process we've just completed. Then we'll pull them all together to let them know what we're going to do with the entire organization and why."

Right now you see clearly, Bob, but there may be a time in the next few months that you may not. In fact, you will probably wonder why we did all of this. When that time comes, and it will come, you will be alone with your choice. It's then that you will need to remember who you really are. Future pace it now, Bob, because you will need it then."

"I understand, Jack, and I'm visualizing as we speak. Let's begin this thing."

The two men shook hands and the transformation of Corporate Insights began.

CONSIDER

- Engaging employees in fleshing out the CEO's Vision broadens and deepens the meaning while creating ownership.

- If you can't trust your employees to create the Mission, then you haven't engaged them in the Vision – the possibility the company is today and in the future.

- The only thing that stops people are their own limiting beliefs.

- There are individual and organizational limiting beliefs. Left unchallenged, each can have a profound effect on organizational performance.

- The organizational model mirrors the human model.

- The collective-ego, sometimes called homeostasis, is a human condition of maintaining equilibrium and a resistance to change. This resistance to change characterizes all self-regulating systems.

- Human entropy is the tendency of people in motion to slow down and forget why they were in motion to begin with.

- CEOing is a 90-day ritual that overcomes the effects of both the collective ego and human entropy while ensuring people remain engaged at every level in the company.

CHAPTER 17

THE SECOND BOARD MEETING

"It's never too late to be what you might have been."
– George Elliot

Phil's plane landed in Oakland at 7:30 A.M.. He walked directly to the shuttle bus and 20 minutes later he was on the BART for the short hop under the Bay to San Francisco. He exited on Montgomery Street and headed to the local CI office on Post Street. Along the way he stopped at Starbucks for a coffee. While Phil was sitting at his table and enjoying the smell of coffee and general good nature of the other customers, he thought about his upcoming meeting with Bob. Phil knew that he had taken a risk with the Board when he so strongly encouraged Bob to work with Jack. None of the other Board members had ever worked with a CEO Coach or gone through a transformational process, so they didn't understand the value of giving Bob time to go through the process. Phil had to hold the Board off from censoring and judging too quickly Bob's initial lackluster performance. The Board was concerned about Bob's flustered, defensive reaction during his first Board meeting the previous week. The Board had been looking for an honest evaluation of where Bob saw the company, but he had seemed to take their questions like an attack, rather than legitimate inquiries. The last thing the Board wanted was another 'lone ranger' CEO, which was their perception of Jim.

Phil felt sure that Jack would have a profound effect on Bob, and when Bob had called him last night, Phil wasn't disappointed. Bob was centered, clear that his past attitude was not very helpful, and ready to talk openly to the Board. Bob described what he had learned during his two days with Jack. "So Phil, what is your Passion and Purpose," asked Bob.

"Thanks for asking," said Phil. "My Passion is *Seize the Day*. My Purpose is *By being open, curious and caring, explore and create new possibilities that generate exciting opportunities for the achievement of wealth and fulfillment for myself and others.*

After hearing Phil's Purpose and Passion statement, it became clear to Bob why Phil decided to leave Atlantic and become a venture capitalist. They now had a common understanding and language, and felt a stronger bond because of it.

Bob returned to San Francisco after his wrap-up meeting with Jack on Sunday morning. He spent the day Monday preparing for the Board meeting and was in the office early on Tuesday morning. Board members began arriving beginning at 9 A.M.. The meeting began promptly at 10 A.M. Unlike the previous meeting this was much less formal. Phil called the meeting to order.

"I'm really glad we could all make it back to San Francisco on such short notice. As you know, Bob took the opportunity to work with a CEO coach, Jack Griffin, to consider both his participation as CEO and to evaluate the direction of the company. The Purpose of today's meeting is to allow Bob to describe his Vision for CI and to gain our input and alignment on the path he has laid out. Phil looked around the room at each Board member, and then said, "Bob, you're up."

Bob stood, walked confidently to the front of the room and took a moment to look each member in the eyes. He went around the table with a smile on his face and was delighted to notice his gesture was easily returned.

"Thank you all for coming together so soon after our last meeting. I recognize that you are busy people and I appreciate the support you are giving me."

Bob took a moment to take a breath.

"The last time we were together I was less than forthcoming. I apologize for that. I know that you all have the best interest of the company at heart and you deserved better. So from now on, as long as you want me to serve as CEO, I promise to be fully open with you."

The group seemed to take a collective breath and settled into their chairs.

"Some of you might be wondering why this big change of attitude. Well, Phil had the wisdom to introduce me to a pretty insightful CEO Coach by the name of Jack Griffin. Our conversation over Friday and Saturday gave me new insights into my own behavior as a leader. I now have a broader perspective on my role, what's important to me both personally and professionally, and what I really want for this company. I'd like to share that with you this morning. I expect you will have questions and suggestions and I welcome them."

There were some raised eyebrows and a few skeptical looks but Bob's comments were mostly received with nodding heads and smiles. Bob began with a quick but candid description of his findings over the previous six weeks.

"In short, the staff at all levels is demoralized and we are unsure of ourselves. I believe this originated at the very top, with both Jim and me. We need to operate as a team, not as two separate entities. Toward that end, I propose that we re-align under a new Vision that engages each and every one of us, including the Board.

Bob began his discussion by placing the flip chart pages he had prepared the previous evening on the walls around the room. He used these charts to describe his plan for engaging and aligning all CI employees. As Bob talked he ran up against all the typical comments about 'soft stuff' not being a strategy that the Board could live with. But this time the Board noticed that Bob just smiled, and said "I understand." And Bob did understand, because he had had the same reservations when he had started to work with Jack. He went on to show how the 'soft stuff' was critical to the results the Board was looking for and how ignoring it would lead them right back into the chaos and uncertainty they were currently experiencing.

As Bob continued to move through the information on the charts he was able to engage the group in deep discussion and he began to get broad agreement – especially as he began to address their desires. When he got to the end of his goals he used Jack's technique of having them mark each item with a T, $ or P and the Board began to understand the wisdom of Bob's approach.

"You were collectively responsible for giving us the life blood of cash to make CI become a viable organization," said Bob. "The only credible way to leverage the cash you've given us, as you can see from the work we've been doing this morning, is to leverage the people of CI and their relationships to move forward and become a fully integrated, fully functioning organization.

"Gentlemen, it is the people, both in this room and in CI's work force who will create CI's success or not. Just as the relationships in this room depend upon having confidence and faith in one another, the same is true for the relationships between CI employees.

"What do I mean when I say relationships are critical to our success? The best way for me to explain is to describe myself before working with Jack. Prior to last week I was driven by fear, lack of trust, and a need to control everything. Leading from this mind set caused me to be defensive and to require a high level of control. It became apparent through my work with Jack that operating out of fear of failure and behaving in a defensive and controlling manner would not bring about the needed changes in CI. For me to serve this Board and lead change at CI in a positive and constructive way, I've had to make some fundamental changes within myself. I believe that many CI employees are operating in the same negative framework as I was, and that we must provide the same opportunity for them to change that I was given. I'll describe how this change process will occur throughout the organization, because I need your commitment and support for it to be successful. But first, I'd like to describe how I think CI must shift its business focus."

This last comment caught the Board by surprise and made them sit a little closer to the table.

"Our entire business proposition is based on providing software that helps our customers identify and manage the most important, mission critical projects across their increasingly distributed organizations. We call what we do enhancing enterprise visibility.

"What I noticed in my work with Jack this past week is that we haven't been using our own software solutions – and we have experienced breakdowns in our own enterprise visibility as a result. Why have we failed to use our own product?"

Bob paused for questions but there were none. Everyone was eager to see where he was going. He continued.

"Then I began thinking, in the entertainment business, to give you an example, the major delivery providers – cable and satellite, and electronics manufacturers – have all been engaged in closing what the entertainment industry calls the 'last mile' into consumer homes. There have been many partial solutions over the past few years, but nothing that has opened up the real potential for the consumer, which has been described as full duplex operation within the home. Full duplex simply means two-way communication at a speed that will allow easy communication.

"In our business, the 'last mile' is getting our users to fully integrate and use our solutions to enterprise visibility. We've been faced with the question of how to do that.

"Then I realized that our enterprise visibility solution is a one-way view built upon the old directive model of business. It allows management to look out, but doesn't do a very good job of allowing teams to look back the other way. Basically, it's based on fear, not possibility. We call it early warning so we won't get blindsided," said Bob.

"I now believe the company that closes the last mile in our business will be the one that creates true enterprise transparency, and actually engages the hearts and minds of its people to want to share what's really going on. That means how we help customers deploy our solutions will have to be expanded from just the technology component, to include a human component as well. Let me explain what I'm talking about here.

"It's no secret that a large part of our software's full capability is routinely left untapped because the users are not engaged or inspired to do anything but the bare minimum. Now, this is true for simple word processing programs as well, it's not just our software. But it's critical for us to more fully engage our users if our solution is going to truly benefit our customers. Now here's the reality: *we don't know how to do that.* In fact we don't even know how to get our own people to use our solution completely.

"So, to engage and inspire our users, we must first be able to engage and inspire our own people. If we can do that, we can design a pre-installation seminar based upon what we learn in the next six months that will set us apart from our competition by transforming our users to our cause – creating enterprise visibility.

"This may sound a bit esoteric to some of you, so let me share a story told to me by Jack Griffin which may illustrate my point a little better.

"Jack had been trying to write a book for some time and it never seemed to get done. So one day during a quiet moment he got down on his knees and almost shouted: So God, do you want me to finish this darned book or what?"

The group laughed at the sight of Bob mimicking Jack on his knee, arms outstretched looking up into the heavens.

"And as he tells it, God told him, just as loudly 'No, Jack, I don't want you to write the book, I want you to be the book.'"

Bob let that sit in the air for a moment, then said. "Jack had to *be* the book first.

"Gentlemen, I am asking for your help in being the book we desire to write together."

"If we want to write the book on enterprise visibility, or as I intend, enterprise transparency, then we must first build it into the culture of our company and learn what it really takes to make it happen within an organization. Let me differentiate the two for you."

Enterprise Visibility	Enterprise Transparency
Our software facilitates a one-way look into client organizations that focuses on high ROI projects. Requires candid input from remote reaches of the organization.	Our software and training facilitates a two-way look throughout the organization into the possibility of generating and supporting high ROI projects that grow people in the process. Requires powerful relationships and candid conversation throughout the organization.

"As you can see this model can be applied to our company as well as our software," Bob concluded.

There was a quiet moment and Bob thought to himself, "Oh boy, they must think I've really lost it." But he just kept smiling and confidently making eye contact. The group looked at one another.

"Jeez, Bob," said Mark Conway, CEO of PT Semiconductor, a very successful specialty semiconductor manufacturer that had continued to grow, even during the semiconductor glut of the recent recession. "This is one hell of a comeback from last week and I've found what you're saying to be very compelling. I agree that engaging people is a big part of the answer, especially with your definition of 'challenged, appreciated, responsible and feeling part of something big.' Engaging people is how I've been able to buck the trend these last two years while the semiconductor industry has been in the dumps. And I've learned some new things this morning that I'll be considering for my own company.

"And while I'm not sure exactly how to get your customers to use CI's software more enthusiastically, I know that no one else in the industry knows this secret either. So I'm intrigued with the possibility of, as you put it, closing the last mile in enterprise visibility. And I love the quote," Mark said, as he put on his reading glasses and looked down at his notes, "*we must be the book before we can write it.* Very powerful!"

Mark's comments opened up a wide-ranging conversation on how the Board could best support Bob in his next steps. They were impressed with Bob's personal turn-around and were encouraged when Bob shared his intention to engage his senior staff immediately and stated that the entire organization would be re-aligned behind and fully engaged in the new Vision and Goals before the end of the current quarter.

The Board had some serious questions when Bob laid out the program timetable and budget, but Bob simply admitted "I understand gentlemen, I initially felt the same way," and went on to demonstrate how a very conservative ROI would pay for the entire program in less than a year.

The Board requested that it be kept informed during each of the 'Be Powerful' process steps and was surprised when Bob invited them to attend the actual events and encouraged them to communicate directly with each group as they went through the program. Having the Board back the program would do a lot to encourage full participation with all of CI's employees.

CONSIDER

- How much closer could you be to your people if you knew each other's Core Values, Purpose and Passion? How would you treat each other differently?

- Honesty goes a long way.

- Openness goes farther.

- Inclusion goes even further.

- Everything in your life begins with you.

- Enterprise visibility is directive and a reaction to the fear of not knowing.

- Enterprise transparency is transformative and inspired by organizational possibility.

- You must *be the book* before you can write the book.

CHAPTER 18

ENGAGING THE LEADERSHIP TEAM

Energy always follows focus

To kick off the Executive Team level of the program, Bob arranged to have his direct reports meet Jack for a half-day introduction to allow them the opportunity to buy in to the process. They were scheduled to get together in Chicago at the Palmer House Hotel on the following Tuesday morning. Bob felt a sense of urgency so he woke up early and took some time to think through how he wanted the meeting to proceed. He didn't want to get bogged down like he had the last few times the entire team got together. He put together an agenda that focused on what he wanted to accomplish, but was more concerned about how the meeting would go. How could he quickly get his staff engaged – and even before that, willing to listen? He intended to talk in a different way than he had in the past. Instead of 'telling' what he wanted and engaging in a fight or getting no response, Bob intended to do a lot of 'asking' and 'coaching,' something new for him and certainly new for his staff.

Bob thought about the last staff meeting just three weeks ago.

A few minutes before the meeting was scheduled to begin, a loud, abusive argument had broken out between Chris Cooper, VP of Software Development and Bill Smith, the new VP of European Operations. Bill, although young and new to the post by only a few weeks, had proven himself to be a fine leader and an excellent technician. He was Bob's number two in Europe and had proven his mettle many times during the preceding year. It was clear from the heated nature of the confrontation that Chris was out of control. Bob had to take both of the Executives quite forcefully out of the room to cool them down.

Bob sure as hell didn't want something like that to happen again. His thoughts returned to this morning's meeting. If he didn't want the bickering and confrontation, what did he want? He took a moment and wrote down his intentions for the meeting.

"I intend that the meeting is open and participatory; that we all learn some new ways of being; that we all leave the meeting excited about what's next for the company; and that we all feel like we can make a difference."

He put his pad and pen down and sat back in his chair, looked up at the ceiling and closed his eyes. "Hmmm," he thought, "how can I get that? Maybe just keep it simple. Just tell the truth about my own recent experiences and share what I hope to get from the meeting." He would use some of Jack's meeting tools.

Bob made it to the Palmer House early to make sure he was there to greet each of his staff. He'd chosen this location for the first half day session because it was convenient for travel and also because he appreciated the calm and welcoming ambience of the meeting rooms.

Bob briefly introduced Jack to the group. He then remarked, "I want you all to notice that today's meeting will be run differently than the ones we've had in the past. In today's meeting Jack and I will ask you to 'think outside of the box' and look at things differently. We will act as coaches and facilitators rather than playing the traditional team leader or boss role.

"I spent some time this morning articulating what I don't want and what I do want to have happen in today's meeting," Bob said as he lifted a blank piece of flip chart paper to reveal this chart.

What I want **for today's meeting**

- We are open and participate
- That we learn some new things
- That we leave excited about
  what's next
- That we feel like we can make
  a difference

"I'm asking all of you to participate in such a way today that together we only focus on what we do want."

Bob couldn't help but smile to himself as he watched the non-verbal responses. He understood well what they could be thinking, as he had a similar response when he first started to work with Jack.

Bob didn't really expect an overwhelming affirmative response so early in the game, so he moved right along.

"To begin our meeting, I'd like to use a process Jack taught me called 'Clearing.' By way of explaining what 'Clearing' is, let me ask how many of you ever attended a meeting where you were distracted by something before the meeting got under way that left you disengaged?"

A few of the group laughed while others expressed their uneasiness by squirming in their chairs.

MANAGING ENERGY

After a short pause, Bob said, "Over the past few weeks I've learned that leading an organization is about managing human energy. Clearing helps to bring the energy level from highly charged and agitated to a calm and open state. As we begin our meeting this morning, I just want us to notice the state of the energy in the room. Or to help us differentiate, perhaps you will recall the state of the energy in our last meeting in New York just three weeks ago."

He let them sit there for a minute, and then asked, "How would you describe the energy in here – anyone?

"It's angry, scattered, defensive and upset," said Nancy Cummings, VP of Professional Services.

"I have to agree," said Neil Coulter, CFO. "And I'd add resigned. Hell we've gotten so used to blow ups or icy silence we just chalk it up to the way things are around here, and," he added, "I guess I've added to the blow ups as much as anyone," relieving some of the pent up tension in the room.

Bob went around the room and made sure everyone 'cleared' by acknowledging how they were feeling or how they read the energy of the room.

Bob had their attention.

Then he came to Chris, who was goading the others simply with his body and facial language. His rolling eyes, tipping his chair back and drumming his fingers on the table clearly indicated his distain for the conversation.

"So Chris, how do you read the energy, or what's going on in the room?" asked Bob.

"Horseshit!" said Chris, "This is all a bunch of happy horseshit and I don't have time for all this woo-woo shit. It all means nothing."

"Okay," said Bob without the slightest sign of irritation. "Thanks for sharing."

There was a muffled laugh in the room from some of the other participants. Chris's response wasn't a surprise and Bob refused to be drawn into a confrontation set off by Chris's negativity and blatant disrespect.

"Chris, would you mind if I asked you a different question?"

"No, not at all," Chris replied as he tipped his chair back into it's normal position, folding his hands in front of him on the table.

Bob looked around the room and continued by saying, "Thanks for your honest input. This clearing process is useful because it let's me know exactly where we are in our relationship. Knowing where you all stand is really a gift because I don't have to waste my time or yours discussing things no one has the slightest intention of following up on. It gives us an honest place to begin. I acknowledge these feelings as being very real – and hopefully you can see how they could get in the way of a successful meeting. So I'm asking you to note that Jack has recorded your feelings on the board, so we know we've been heard, and simply move to 'neutral' so that we have a chance at moving from what we 'don't want' to what we 'do want,'" he said as he pointed to his flip chart page.

DON'T WANT VERSUS DO WANT

"Just as I asked myself, *'What do I want from this meeting today?'* I'd like each of you to answer that same question. Bob then brought his attention back to Chris.

"So Chris," said Bob, "What is it you really want?"

"I don't want you guys telling me that my people aren't doing a great job. My team is busting their asses every day and every day you guys change things and cause even more fires!" he said pointing at the group.

Bob glanced at Jack as he began to sit down, signaling Jack to take the ball. The transition was smooth – like they had been working together forever.

"Chris," said Jack, "this may seem like a small thing, but it can make all the difference in the world," as he finished copying Chris's words onto the chart pad. "Rather than state what you *don't want*, I'd like you to state what you do *want*."

Chris turned red and said, "What the hell is the difference between what I do and don't want? I'm a problem solver, and when there is something wrong I call a spade a spade."

"Do you want to know the difference?" asked Jack. "I mean, would you be interested in learning another way to get the things you want, a way that's 100% more effective and efficient with little energy expended and certainly a lot less stress?

"And the rest of you, how many of you would like to have more results with less stress – anyone?"

Jack put his hand up looking for involvement and patiently stood there with his hand in the air. Slowly, all the other hands went up except for Chris, who, although he looked more interested, still had an air of defensiveness.

"There are some valuable lessons to be learned from this morning if we are open to them. The first is to realize that energy always follows focus, and leadership is about managing the energy of the organization. The negative energy we described in our 'clearing' certainly won't contribute to CI's growth and success, so as leaders we must be aware of the effect of negative energy and have the skills to change it. And the second is to understand that *focusing on what we want* is more powerful than *focusing on what we don't want.*"

With that, Jack turned and faced Chris.

"So Chris, if there was something you really wanted from your peers, what would it be?"

Chris shifted around in his seat for a minute, and then he said "I guess it would be that we work together in such a way that we are more supportive of one another and there are no surprises.

"Fine," said Jack, writing down Chris's last words, underlining the last two "But is there something you want, beyond no surprises?"

"Hum. Well, I want my team to be supported and have what we need to do our jobs when we need it."

Again, Jack captured Chris's comments.

There was silence as the group absorbed the implications of Chris's shift from 'don't want' to 'do want.'

"Does anyone notice any difference here?"

"Yes. Chris's being positive and cooperative rather than negative and defensive," said Bill Peters, VP of Sales & Marketing. Bill's comments were surprising because the two were such good friends. Chris didn't seem to mind.

"Good," said Jack, "What if you could depend upon each other to always focus the organization's energy on what it wants, rather than on what it doesn't want? What are the implications of such an organization?"

Chris spoke first, surprising everyone.

"The focus, and therefore all of our energy, would always be on creating what we want..." he said.

"Yes?" supported Jack.

"...and we would save ourselves a ton of work and stress as well," Chris concluded thoughtfully.

"I want to acknowledge Chris for being a good sport and working this through. We all know this shift isn't just about Chris, is it?" continued Jack, "It's about all of us."

Heads nodded in agreement.

"Our work today is about changing the context in which we choose to live our lives and run this company. So far I think we can safely say that the context in which Corporate Insights has been running is one of fear, uncertainty and doubt. How many would agree with that?"

Slowly, all hands went up.

"How many of you would like to be able to shift the context of things at will? To be able to shift conversations, meetings and organizational performance from reactive to creative, from negative to positive very quickly?"

All the hands went up again, this time more readily.

Jack saw Bob's hand signal that it was time for a break and handed the meeting back to Bob.

"I want to thank you all for your support in this morning's meeting and for so readily engaging in this conversation. So far it's been quite different from our usual agenda," said Bob with a smile. "Let's take a 15 minute break before we get started on what's next."

As Bob walked out on the patio with Jack and a fresh cup of coffee, he savored the experience of the morning. He would have never dreamed that the simple act of stating what he did want, rather than focusing on what he didn't want would be such a powerful strategy. He was really looking forward to the second half of the meeting. A feeling he had rarely experienced in the past.

As people settled into their chairs after the break, Bob went over to his "don't want/want" chart, and spoke aloud the thoughts he had had during the break.

"If someone would have told me that negative energy and focus could be changed in a little less than forty-five minutes, I would have said 'in your dreams.' Yet we have done that this morning," said Bob as he pointed to the chart. "And I want to thank all of you for your candor and support. What we did this morning is just a small glimpse into the work we will continue to do, with ourselves individually, and together, on behalf of our people. To help you get a picture of where we are going, I'd like to take some time to describe my experiences since I was appointed to the Acting CEO position."

Bob candidly shared his impressions of the organization during his travels to different locations, how he acted during his first Board meeting, and described his meeting with Jack. When he was describing his work with Jack, Bob posted more charts, including his Purpose and Passion statement, his Values and his From-To sheets and his Vision statement for CI.

Finally, Bob shared the very different outcome of the second Board meeting. "I've arranged for each of you to experience the Personal Visioning process I just went through. I have the Board's blessing to move forward with this program. It's going to take more than just a little faith in ourselves and one another to go through this. But I believe this work is fundamental to CI's success. I am asking for your support and commitment."

Bob stood there. Smiling.

"You have my support Bob," said Nancy.

One by one, Bob's direct reports acknowledged their support by either nodding their heads or with a verbal affirmation.

Chris was last. He and Bob locked eyes. "Okay Bob, you've got me. Besides, I wouldn't want to wreck this little bonding moment you've got going here," said Chris with a wry grin.

"Thank you," said Bob. "I'm looking forward to seeing each of you on the second day of your Visioning Retreat.

EXECUTIVE VISIONING

Over the next two weeks each VP met with Jack and his team for a two-day Visioning Session. Just like Bob, the executives focused on their individual Values, Purpose/Passion, and Limiting Beliefs, while the second day clarified strategic intention for their individual departments. At the end of day two, Bob joined them. The individual shared his or her Purpose and Passion statement, Core Values, Limiting Beliefs and explored the strategic implications of his or her individual department in light of Bob's new focus. This exchange was meaningful because it provided considerable insight into one another and, where needed, a realignment of priorities. At the end of this session, both the Direct Report and Bob had a clear understanding of what they expected from one another. More importantly, they had each other's commitment.

From the very beginning of the executive retreats the feedback Bob received was delightfully positive. The evening after her first session, Nancy Cummings e-mailed Bob.

"I was reluctant to participate in this new process, thinking it would just be a waste of time, but after the first day I have to admit it was unlike anything I've ever done before. It was focused on me and my needs, not the company's, which, I don't mind telling you, was both unexpected and appreciated. The Purpose & Passion section really gave me more of a solid foundation for my decision-making process, one that I hadn't fully realized was there before. It made a profound difference to me, Bob. Thank you. I look forward to working with you tomorrow from an entirely new level of Purpose & Passion, not panic."

Bob smiled as he read the e-mail. It was a good sign. Nancy was a heavyweight and if she saw the value in the process then the others would probably see it as well.

As the days progressed, the feedback he was receiving was heartening, with Bob receiving e-mails and telephone calls from each executive detailing their unusual experience. And with each completion the others, still waiting their turn, began to show a genuine excitement. They actually looked forward to their retreat and began sharing the anticipation with their directs.

"Imagine," thought Bob, "an entire team in touch with who they really are and willing and able to make decisions and have conversations from the heart as well as the head. No more covering asses."

LEADERSHIP TEAM CHARTER

When the last VP had completed his individual Visioning Process, they again got together in Chicago at the Palmer House and again Bob was at the door to welcome them. As they entered the room they noticed seven chairs arranged in a circle. Jack directed them to take a seat.

After clearing, in which each shared their Visioning experience in some detail and how much they had learned from the process, Jack asked each to introduce him or herself as their Purpose and Passion and, from that place, share what their commitment was to the people of Corporate Insights. It was a moving experience.

When they finished, Bob stood.

"Our task today is three-fold. The first, which we've just

fulfilled, was to put aside our Egos and introduce ourselves as who we really are. In the future you can count on me to speak to that part of you. I am committed to the truth of who we really are, and not our five-year-old Ego selves."

The entire group laughed out loud.

"And I expect you to relate to me that way as well. Because, as I'm sure Jack has told you, we are entering into the second phase of knowing who you are, and that's self-mastery. We've all had many years acting out of our Egos and I don't expect that to go away any time soon, but I do expect progress. And I think we can all support each other in this regard."

"Second, we must create a Leadership Charter. This document will state how we, as the leadership of this company, will behave toward one another and our people in the future. I don't have any preconceived notion of what it will say exactly or what form it will take, but this I do know. It is not about the content of what we do. Rather, it's about the context of what we do.

"Finally, we must plan how we are going to get all 442 of our people through the Corporate Insights *Be Powerful* program and demonstrate measurable results to the Board and to ourselves within the next 90 days."

The last announcement created a quite a stir.

Bob smiled, and said "I told you it would take some mastery."

And the group laughed out loud again.

"Jack has been through many of these programs, so we are in good hands. After spending two days with him and his people I think you'll agree."

The group nodded their agreement.

"So, to begin our next task I'm going to ask Jack to again review with us the difference between Directive and Transformative organizations. Then we'll discuss the implications of this for CI, as well for us as the leadership team when we make the shift." It was clear from Bob's body language and tone of voice that he was committed to the shift. He was exuding confidence and his team responded.

After a few individual and team exercises the group quickly

articulated a Leadership Team Charter that carried the spirit and intention of the Corporate Insights Vision *Be Powerful.*

> **Corporate Insights Leadership Charter**
>
> We are the Corporate Insights Leadership team. Our Charter is to fully engage each other and our people in the powerful execution of our stated Vision: Be Powerful. We will know we are truly engaging our people when employees report, through an independent employee survey, at least a 10% improvement per quarter in the degree to which employees feel challenged, appreciated, responsible and part of something meaningful until at least 90% engagement is reached.

When they felt the charter was finished, Jack asked them to sign and date it. They were excited to do it. When they were done the group went to a well-deserved lunch.

When they returned they set out to create the timetable for bringing the rest of the company through the *Be Powerful* program. Jack shared his experience and answered questions, the most important of which had to do with what Jack and his team would be doing with the employees for three days.

Jack uncovered a flip chart page that they had all seen on the first day of their Visioning sessions and began to explain the process that the companywide initiative would follow.

"On the first day, your people will understand who they are and how to be more of that in their lives. They will begin to let go of their limiting beliefs. On the second, they will begin to understand and appreciate each other and begin the process of building powerful relationships with each other. And on the third day, they will come into alignment with the Vision. Along the way, they will articulate and agree upon a set of company Values and a Code of Honor that will guide our collective behavior and, as key stakeholders, will develop the Corporate

> **Leadership Secrets**
>
> 1. To be Powerful in your life, you must first understand and master yourself
>
> 2. To be Powerful with others, you must first understand humanity and master relationships
>
> 3. To be Powerful in the world, you must learn to co-create and master a game worth playing

Mission."

When one of the VPs questioned letting employees develop the Values, Code of Honor and Mission Statement, Jack simply smiled and deferred to Bob.

"This is one of the most important questions you could ask," acknowledged Bob, "I know I had a lot of trouble with it myself. In fact, in questioning it, I ended up learning a lot about myself. But suffice it to say the exercise will be an important lesson in empowerment. And besides, each of you will be on one of the employee teams that define what the Mission is."

Jack privately reflected that Bob had really learned a powerful lesson. And as Bob continued sharing his experience with the question and the logic behind bringing people into the process, the group aligned with the approach.

In the end, the group decided there would be two major efforts, one for directors, managers and supervisors, and another for the employees of the organization. Jack confirmed that each one of the VPs would be required to attend the last two days of one of the three-day sessions as an ordinary participant. This would demonstrate leadership commitment to the program, and also allow them to experience first-hand what the group experienced. They all readily agreed.

They also made the decision to cover each other so that all 42 directors, managers and supervisors could be sent to Atlanta for the three-day introduction to *Being Powerful*.

Bob was really encouraged at how engaged everyone was.

It was a larger task to figure out how to get all of the employees through the program. After much discussion they decided to split the entire company, all 442 of them into 4 employee groups of 100 or so – with the one manager group of 42. They created a timetable to complete the *Be Powerful* program in five weeks.

Throughout the planning, Bob couldn't help but notice that some of the executives were still referring to PDQ as a separate entity so he took the opportunity make the "seamless integration of PDQ" a key deliverable of the process. All agreed.

Three-day manager and employee retreats were scheduled for Atlanta, Los Angeles, Dallas, New York, London and Bombay – now known as Mumbai – the latter only after a good deal of deliberation. Mumbai was a group of 30 Indian contract programmers and some felt it was a lot of expense to include them in the *Be Powerful* process. However Sangi Mehta, the project manager on the ground in India, made an impassioned plea to the Leadership Team that this important group should be included.

In the end, it was Chris who insisted that, to walk the talk, everyone had to be embraced and brought into the new culture of *Being Powerful*, and that included the people in India. The group bought in to the argument and India was in.

In order to demonstrate sensitivity to the high number of hours people were working already, Bob was adamant that weekends and holidays not be used for either travel time or the *Be Powerful* process itself, so all the meetings were scheduled for Tuesdays, Wednesdays and Thursdays.

The team would make it a point to transmit this accommodation to the employees. This was going to be an enormous investment. It was a good thing the Board was behind him, Bob thought time and again, as the budget for this transformation was more than $500,000 plus travel, food and lodging. "By the time we're through this will cost close to $800,000," thought Bob, "but unlike Sarbanes-Oxley, which cost over a million dollars to implement and did nothing for productivity, *Be Powerful* will give us a fast start and a fast ROI." Bob had used that as part of the argument with the Board and, surprisingly, resenting the seeming waste of money on compliance with government regulations, the Board endorsed the *Be Powerful* program but requested the cost be spread over two quarters. Jack agreed to the accommodation.

CONSIDER

- Leading individuals and organizations is about managing human energy.

- Energy follows focus.

- Our Ego selves will always tend to focus on what we don't want, generating negative energy and leading us in unproductive directions.

- Our Purpose selves will always focus on what we do want – on the possibility of a situation – generating positive, encouraging energy.

- Leaders come from their Purpose, in alignment with the organization's Purpose.

- Clearing at the beginning of a meeting helps dissipate negative energy and focus attention on the topic at hand.

- Clearing at the end of a meeting helps determine the degree of follow-through you can expect from the group.

- The ability to speak to a person's stated Purpose and Passion opens a powerful channel to their Spirit.

- The ability to speak to an organization's stated Purpose unleashes the exponential power of Passion.

- Leadership is distinct from management. Management is about maintaining the status quo – about survival. Leadership is about growth and development. Manage process and lead people.

- We are living in an age when each individual has enormous potential for good in the world. Leaders can unleash this positive potential by the raising each individual's awareness of who they really are in the world.

- Empowering people means giving them hope and lifting

them out of cynicism.

- Contrary to conventional wisdom, Hope is a strategy.

- Empowering people requires preparing them to succeed and then giving them the space to do so.

- If your people aren't empowered or don't have the tools to write the Mission, Values and Code of Honor for the company, how does this reflect on you as a leader?

- The investment to transform people is far less than the price of continuing to let them live in fear, uncertainty and doubt, and lowering productivity.

CHAPTER 19

THE MANAGER TEAM RETREAT

"A competitive world has two possibilities for you: you can lose or,
if you want to win, you can change."
— Lester C. Thurow

On the first day, judging from how many were late, it was clear that quite a few of the participants didn't want to be there. It turned out that, although the VPs had shared their recent Visioning experiences with their managers, something seemed to have been lost in the translation. "Joe's Kid," thought Jack. No matter how excited their bosses were, several of the managers were still listening to the VPs through their Ego filter, so their sentiment was, "Yeah, right!" However, he also observed that many of the participants were more curious than skeptical.

The 9 A.M. start time came and went. At Jack's suggestion, there was a last-minute flurry of phone calls by a few of the managers to find missing participants and get them into the room. Everyone was talking, with a few beginning to complain that the facilitator should have started on time. This was all part of the process.

The seating was theater style. There were flip chart easels at the front of the room on each side. There was also a conference speaker-phone sitting alone on a small draped table at the front of the room. As soon as the last missing person took their seat – with more than a little fanfare and ribbing – and before Jack introduced himself or his team, the phone came to life. It was loud because it was hooked into the meeting room's speaker system. Jack let it ring until it had captured everyone's attention. He walked over and hit the 'on' button and said, "Hello Bob, we're all here." Bob said hello and Jack, using pantomime, led the entire group in returning the greeting. Bob was silent for a moment on the other end of the phone, and then he said:

Imagine[10] a world
where people are amazingly effective
as individuals and as members of teams.
Where they understand the business
and how they impact it.
Where they live where they want,
work where and when they want
and are powerfully effective.
Imagine a world
of global relationships
where prosperity and teamwork
replace cultural strife.
Where prosperity is driven by the right ideas,
the right efforts
and the right measures,
all focused on making a contribution,
to one another and our customers
rather than personal agendas
and departmental fiefdoms.
Imagine, *what could we be?*

Bob let the words sink in a bit, then, he said, "These were the words of our founder, Jim Wellington, who was one of my early mentors while I was at Deloitte. At the time when I first heard these words I didn't understand Jim's passion. Now I do. At the time I thought his sentiments were fluffy and pie in the sky. Now I don't.

"I believe it is our destiny, yours and mine, to help facilitate the kind of environment that Jim described in his poem, *Imagine*. I believe it is our destiny to lead the world in facilitating effective enterprise visibility, and ultimately, as we learn more, authentic enterprise transparency. But to begin, to actually help our clients create enterprise visibility and manage even the most complex

---

[10] The poem Imagine by the late George Van Ness, used with permission.

projects to fruition, we must first do it within our own company. We must become the future we desire to have, we must become the book we wish to write.

"Over the next few days you are going to experience yourselves and each other differently. Together you will discover a new possibility for yourselves and for our organization. And along the way some of you will question what all this has to do with business. I know I did.

"Don't be afraid to question, and don't be afraid to listen to one another. Because, built on the shoulders of what we've already achieved, you are the ones we are calling upon to invent a new possibility for the company. I invite you to participate like the quality of our lives depends on it – because the quality of our lives does depend on your commitment to this effort.

"Thank you for being here. Thank you for your participation. And enjoy your time together. Jack, they are all yours."

Jack thanked Bob and again orchestrated a rousing "Goodbye Bob!" from the group.

When the group settled down, Jack took a moment to look at each and every director, manager and supervisor in the room. There were forty-two of them.

Jack raised his right hand as he asked the group, *"How many of you would like to get up each morning more excited than you've been in years?"* He let the question hang in the air, catching the group unaware of what to do. He just smiled. And with his hand still in the air, asked, *"How many of you would like to dramatically improve the relationships in your life, both at work and at home?"* People caught on and, one-by-one, began putting their hands up, answering the question for themselves. *"How many of you would like to know that you're making a difference in the world in everything you do?"* By this time most of the hands were up. "And," Jack said loudly, *"How many of you would like to make a lot more money and have a lot more time off?"* With the last question all the hands were up and agreement was amplified by some hoots and hollers. "Well, you've come to the right place…" and for the next three days Jack delivered on that promise. The management team would never be the same.

CONSIDER

- "Joe's Kid" is a real phenomenon that disempowers us all.

- Our automatic Ego-selves keep everyone and everything in our lives in a nice, neat box. They hold us back. Just as we hold others back.

- Until people become attuned to their Purpose and Passion, they will remain slaves to the reaction of their Ego.

- Transforming an entire enterprise at the same time gives the leader an enormous opportunity to dramatically reduce the "Surprise Factor" in business by unleashing the exponential power of Purpose and Passion.

- Imagine a world where people are amazingly effective. Imagine what we could be.

- What is your destiny?

- Would you like to get up each morning more excited than you have ever been before?

- Would you like to dramatically improve the relationships in your life, both at work and at home?

- Would you like to know, without any shadow of a doubt, that you are making a difference in the world in everything you do?

- Would you like to make a lot more money and have a lot more time off?

- What's necessary is that we learn how to authentically engage people in the lives they already want: to be challenged, appreciated, responsible and part of a game worth playing.

CHAPTER 20

CREATING EMPLOYEE CRITICAL MASS

DAY ONE

Engaging people requires that you care about them.

The first group of ninety-two employees came together in Los Angeles exactly five days after their managers left the Atlanta retreat. They also demonstrated a healthy level of skepticism, although, in fairness, London would beat all the other groups in the skeptical/resistant department. After all, they had just completed the time-consuming continuous improvement program the year before with nothing much to show for all the hype and initial flurry of activity. The Indian contingent joined the employees in London in order to engender a closer relationship between the two groups and added a valuable dimension to the dialog.

Early on, the general consensus among the technical and administrative staff was that this would probably be just another one of those stupid exercises that never changes anything. There was added resentment because of all the work that would be piling up while they were in the training.

There were a few staff members, however, who pointed out that the VPs and managers actually seemed to be working better together. Some were acting downright different, even smiling and genuinely asking for an opinion. "When the managers came back from Atlanta," said one engineer, "they were way too happy for me. I don't know what's up with them. When we asked what was going on they just smiled and told us, 'You'll see!' No matter how we pressed them, no one gave it up." The overall attitude of this first group of staff was 'wait and see.'

As with the manager's group, the conference phone sitting on a table at the front of the room rang when everyone was in the room and seated. Jack let it ring, getting everyone's attention. Bob delivered his speech again and the process began.

Jack raised his right hand as he asked the group, *"How many of you would like to get up each morning more excited than you've been in years?"* As he did with their managers the week before, Jack just let the question hang in the air, catching the group unaware of what to do. He just smiled. And with his hand still in the air, asked, *"How many of you would like to dramatically improve the relationships in your life, both at work and at home?"* People caught on and, one by one, began putting their hands up, answering the question for themselves. *"How many of you would like to know that you're making a difference in the world in everything you do?"* By this time most of the hands were up. *"And,"* Jack said loudly, *"how many of you would like to make a lot more money and have a lot more time off?"* With the last question many of the hands were up and people were animated.

"Well, you've come to the right place..."

From the very beginning the group was engaged, laughing and poking fun at one another. Within the first hour it was clear that this wasn't going to be an ordinary seminar.

"Today is going to be all about you! Tomorrow will be about your relationship with the person sitting next to you. And our third day will focus on creating a game worth playing. So let me ask you, how many of you want to get the absolute most out of our time together?" The majority of hands went up. "Great, so who can tell me some of the ways we learned everything that we know as adults up to this point in our lives?" Some hands went up. "Good. Yes, Joseph?"

"We read!" said Joseph.

"Excellent. How else do we learn? Bert?"

"We watch other people!"

"Great. How else? Sandra?"

By engaging the participants, Jack got to the point he wanted to make. "We learn what we learn through our senses; we hear things, we see things and we feel things," said Jack. "Another way to say this is that we learn verbally, through modeling others and through direct experience. There is a saying, what we hear, we forget, what we see, we remember, and what we experience we become. So, which do you think is the best way to learn?"

"To experience," shouted the group.

"And how can you ensure you will get the experience you desire?"

"By participating," shouted someone in the group.

"Excellent, so how many of you are willing to participate 100%?"

By now the noise level had risen to an acceptable roar. All of the hands were in the air. And there was a sense of expectation.

"So, are you ready to get started?" Jack yelled at the top of his lungs.

"Yes," the group screamed back.

"Excellent!" yelled Jack.

Jack had them choose a partner for the day. He explained that as partners they were to assist each other in discovering who they really were under their Ego-masks. Some of the partnerships were unlikely, but everyone agreed to suspend judgment for the day and give a genuine effort to the process.

The day was packed from 8 A.M. until 8 P.M., but most commented on how the day had flown by. By the time they left for dinner that evening, each person in the group had articulated their individual Values, Unique Abilities, Purpose and Passion and, in the process, learned a great deal about themselves and one another. But most importantly, for the first time in their lives they distinguished their Ego and Purpose and experienced the power of authentic choice.

Day Two

On the morning of the second day something unexpected happened. Everyone, all 92 of the participants, were ready to begin 15 minutes before the official start time of 8 A.M.. Standard operating procedure at work was just the opposite – meetings typically started 15 minutes late.

"How many of you know that the best way to remember something is to review it within 24 hours of learning it?" asked Jack. Most of the hands went up in the air. "Excellent. I want you to pair up and I want you to review everything we did yesterday. Use all the charts on the walls to take one another through the day. Are you ready to do that?"

"Yes!" shouted the group. "Then begin!" said Jack.

After twenty minutes, Jack called them all together for another assignment.

"I'm going to give you an impossible task. I want you to take all 92 of these chairs and arrange them into a perfect circle. You have one minute. Go."

The group startled themselves when they accomplished the feat in 33 seconds and broke into roaring applause when the time was announced.

When they were all seated in the circle Jack had them go around and introduce themselves using their Purpose & Passion statements. There were two instructions. The first was to stand when they shared their Purpose and Passion. And the second was to remain standing through any applause. Then Jack gave them instruction in how to applaud. "I want you to think of a time when you were either at or watching a sporting event and your team scored the winning touchdown, home run, basket, goal, it doesn't matter. I just want to have the people next door to us to go deaf. Am I perfectly clear?"

After a few dry runs, Jack had them at optimal cheering volume and the introductions began.

When the introductions were over, many of the participants commented that they could recognize the other person in their statements, which made them feel aligned with their own Purpose. Others said they felt they could get behind any one of the Purpose statements; even though each was unique, each was a worthy contribution. And still others, when faced with genuine acknowledgement, were simply moved to tears, so seldom had they ever been acknowledged so powerfully.

"We, all of us, simply want to be challenged, appreciated, responsible and part of something meaningful. How may of you would agree with that statement?" asked Jack.

All of the hands went up. And Jack could see in the collective that he was hitting home – tapping into real, authentic desire.

"But that's not what we get, Jack,' said Jeremy Fong, an engineer with the development group. "What we get are death marches, blame, projects that we're working on pulled and given to someone else with no explanation, and hey, how are we supposed to be excited about the future when our leader up and quits with no explanation?"

The group was loudly engaged.

"Thank you, Jeremy, "acknowledged Jack. "How many of you agree with him?"

All the hands went up with a corresponding loud verbal agreement.

"And how many of you want death marches, blame and no explanation?"

None of the hands went up. "Of course not," said Jack.

"But how many of you want to be challenged, appreciated, responsible and part of something meaningful?"

All the hands went up.

"And what do you believe the management team wants?" Jack asked.

There was chaos for a few minutes with many differing views, none overly generous, about what management wanted from them. When the group quieted down, Jack asked them to find a partner and over the lunch break, discuss why things were the way they were if none of them wanted it to be that way.

When the group returned from lunch, Jack introduced them to the impact their beliefs have on them and the organization by handing out a sheet with the top 50 limiting beliefs at Corporate Insights. He asked them to rate each of the limiting beliefs on a scale of 1-10. One of the participants stated that she didn't want to be given a list of generic beliefs. She pushed Jack to add entries to the list from the group. Jack agreed to her request, and then explained that the 50 Limited beliefs on the list were collected from CI employees during telephone interviews the week before. Many of the participants in the room verified the survey.

Limiting Beliefs at Corporate Insights

1. Remote, direct management of employees does not work.
2. It's no use following process because it doesn't work anyway.
3. If you don't inflate a customer problem it won't get any attention.
4. Our products are for customers, not for us.
5. I can't trust anyone here. I can't depend upon existing resources.
6. It doesn't matter how hard you work, there is favoritism here.
7. People are not accountable here.
8. There are no cross-functional teams here, it's us versus them.
9. People are closed, there is little acceptance for new ideas.
10. There is little follow-through on good ideas.
11. We can't trust management to follow through, they can't execute.
12. We are totally focused on profit to the detriment of creativity.
13. People are staying primarily because the job market is so bad.
14. The management team doesn't care about its people.
15. There is no advancement track at Corporate Insights.
16. Technical support is a dead-end job.
17. I have no confidence in Sales.
18. We don't have enough money to survive long-term.
19. Engineering is sub-standard.
20. Account managers aren't managing clients well enough.
21. MIS isn't very talented, nor are they doing their jobs.
22. I don't have the power to effect real change.
23. I can't hand-off to other teams because they just don't have the skills.
24. We'll give up quality and function to meet a deadline.
25. There is a lack of clear direction at every level.

26. Support escalates items prematurely.
27. Development is reluctant to be fully open and honest.
28. When shit happens, we have to find the guilty party.
29. We are not totally up front with the customer.
30. For a small company there is an unhealthy amount of politics.
31. People will not change.
32. People's perceptions of one another will not change.
33. The company is not focused.
34. The executive team politics are so bad you need to be careful.
35. Management is disconnected from the rest of the company.
36. Departments work against each other and that won't change.
37. Work is hard.
38. Middle management has no power.
39. The company will not share decision-making and will not let people in on what's really happening in time for them to contribute ideas.
40. We have to do exactly what customers want whenever they ask for it.
41. I only have to know my job to be successful here.
42. CI is never going to go make it really big.
43. No one is driving the vision.
44. We don't have a plan.
45. Custom versions for each customer are necessary to keep the business.
46. There is no trust for the executive team, they are out of integrity.
47. Marketing is a hot potato and nobody believes in it.
48. There is inadequate training for the requirements.
49. We make customers happy to the detriment of our long-term health.
50. To be successful, we have to prioritize the company before our families, our health or our personal interests.

When Jack was done with the review there was no need to add any more to the list. The average employee held 36 of the 50 limiting beliefs with an average emotional intensity score of 7 out of 10. "We will act or we will not act depending on how we feel," said Jack, "and all progress depends on taking action." When they completed the exercise, the participants understood how all the negative energy was dramatically affecting morale and how departments interacted with each other. And how that negative energy adversely affected their performance. The results of the *Virtual CEO* survey that compared the company against the top best business practices clearly humbled most of the participants. They realized that this was not just a tool to complain about management, but, rather, the score reflected their collective results. They were responsible.

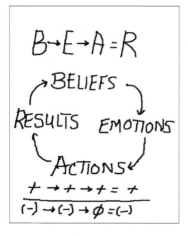

During the day Jack and his team brought the group through a series of exercises that helped them recognize the truth about the organization and one another – they saw that no one went to work to do a bad job – and they were able to let go of the majority of the 50 limiting beliefs. Those Limiting Beliefs that remained were simply displayed on a flip chart at the front of the room and appreciated for their sheer endurance. They would be gone by the end of the third day.

THE RELATIONSHIP FORMULA

The group participated in discussions and exercises that continued to give them glimpses of each other and establish more and more common ground – the first step to creating powerful relationships.

"Sometimes, creating common ground may require chunking all the way up to just being human. And sometimes that's enough, especially when you know from personal experience that being human can be hard work," explained Jack. "It isn't easy being us, is it?"

Jack let that hang in the air.

"The second step in creating powerful relationships is to know what's expected. Mostly, this is where relationships start to fall apart before they even begin because it never occurs to us to ask the boss for clarification because we don't want to appear stupid. Or to ask what she expects from us in our jobs. And you know, it doesn't dawn on us as leaders to ask our people what they expect either.

> **Relationship Formula**
>
> 1. Establish Common Ground
> 2. Know what's expected
> 3. Know where you stand
> 4. Have the courage to ask numbers 2 and 3*
>
> *This may require you step into your personal power just to summon the courage to ask

"The third and most crucial step to creating powerful relationships is to find out where you stand in the relationship. To do that just ask how is it going. Considering you probably never asked what's expected to begin with, number three becomes exponentially harder, because of a basic fear of the potential bad news."

Jack let that sink in for a moment. Then he said, "So the fourth component of a relationship is courage. Having the courage to engage in the relationship requires the willingness to ask how it's going. And that's not easy sometimes. So, I'm about to show you something amazing. I'm going to show you how to access your personal power in any situation, no matter how stressful. Would that be useful?"

The group was enthusiastic and responded with a very loud "Yes!"

A Board member attending the retreat was shocked at how engaged the people were and made a note to speak with Jack at the break. "Do employees always react this positively? Have we been squandering all this energy all along?"

"Very good," continued Jack, "but before I answer, I want to share a story with you. A few years ago we were working with the

Metropolitan Transit Authority of a large east coast city. There were over ten thousand people involved and the agency was in turmoil. There had been three CEOs in one year and we were hired to bring some stability to the organization. That's where I first met an HR manager named Harold Johnson. Harold was the latest of a string of HR managers who had cycled through, and he felt he was soon to be the next to go if something didn't change. I'll never forget Harold because he used what I'm about to show you so powerfully that he's now the V.P. of that department and reports directly to the new CEO."

There were a few looks of skepticism in the group.

"Would anyone here like to know what he did?"

"Yes," said the group.

"When we did Harold's Visioning session, just like we did yours yesterday, his peak experience was catching a winning touchdown when he was in college, some 15 years earlier. Harold described it as being a slow-motion time warp where the only thing he heard was his breath, where he just ran out for the pass, put his two hands up to the side of his head," Jack demonstrated the move, "and the ball was just there. He never looked back to see if it was coming because he just knew it would be there. It was like poetry in motion he said. *And the crowd went wild!*" said Jack with some pantomime.

"But that's not the end of the story. Three months later, at their first 90-day review, and after Harold was promoted for the first time because of all the progress they had made, one of his colleagues came up to me in the hall at a break."

'Jack, he said, 'I've been meaning to ask you something, maybe you know the answer.'

'Sure,' I said, 'how can I help you?'

'Ever since you were last here, every time Harold walks into a meeting, especially with the top brass, he does this,' and he demonstrated putting his hands up to the side of his head."

The group laughed.

"What do you think Harold was doing?" Jack asked the group, "Anyone?"

"He was catching the ball again?" suggested one of the participants.

"Yes, but think about it, why would Harold mimic catching the ball when he went into meetings, especially with the brass?"

"Because he was accessing his personal power." said a young woman from finance.

"Exactly. And that's what I want to teach you right now – how to access your personal power any time and anywhere by creating an anchor and then triggering it when necessary."

By the end of the second day, the group was profoundly related – to themselves and one another. Their clearing included many of the participants asking if they could get copies of some of the exercises to use with their spouses and kids. "Absolutely, feel free to share the exercise with as many of your family members as you wish," agreed Jack, and he directed his assistant to make printed material available at the back of the room.

DAY THREE

They began the third day with another review. Then Jack brought them all together and said, "On the first day we found *ourselves*. Yesterday we found *each other*. Today, we're going to *create a sustainable game worth playing together*. How many of you would like to do that?" said Jack, again with his hand up in the air.

By this time the group was fully engaged and looking forward to what was next. They responded with a resounding "YES!" with a room full of hands in the air.

Jack began by introducing Bob's Corporate Vision (see Appendix A) and asked the group to individually write down a few implications of having such a Vision. The results were inspiring, as people explored the myriad of possibilities. They explored what *Be Powerful* meant to themselves as individuals, to themselves as teams and to themselves as a company. And they expanded their thinking to include customers and vendors alike. Bob's Vision was coming alive.

Next, Jack shared the Leadership Charter (see appendix B) and again, asked the group what that meant to them. "I can't believe our

VPs came up with this," said one participant. The comment got everyone to laugh. They were beginning to get hopeful.

Then, Jack handed out a set of Corporate Values drafted by their directors, managers and supervisors in Atlanta the week before. "These are a set of corporate Values your managers drafted in Atlanta. They are given to you as a foundation only, and the management team has unanimously empowered you to add to them or modify them in any way that you feel will make them clearer and better serve the entire company."

To provide the opportunity for ninety-two people to genuinely participate in discussing and revising the values, Jack broke them into groups of five and six each and assigned two values to each group. There were many groups with the same two values.

"Each group will have two values to consider and comment on. You will also review the entire list of seven to see if anything is missing that you feel absolutely must be on the list. If there is a value you wish to add, you must write down the value, define it fully and agree as a group that it is to be presented to the larger group. Each group must elect a facilitator and a presenter. Each group can add only one new value. At the end of the exercise you will be presenting your input to the larger group."

Many participants expressed their surprise at how efficient this process was – expecting to be arguing fine details all day. They were also amazed, upon first glance, at how good the values drafted by the managers looked, and yet with thought could be enhanced by their group.

Jack explained that the next group would use their updated work as their draft and the process would be repeated, so that literally every person would have had a hand in creating these new guiding principles.

There were a few participants who were offended that they would be asked for their opinion and then make it open to others to change. That simply gave Jack the opportunity to share his definition of empowerment. When the last group finished its work in London, there were eight core values. (See appendix D)

After a break they were introduced to the concept of a Code of

Honor[11], also drafted by the managers in Atlanta. This document detailed how the individuals would behave toward one another and what to do if some didn't. By now the group was operating at a very high level and feeling like they were making a powerful difference.

"All day you have been experiencing what it is to be empowered. But now we are going to do something that has never been done before," announced Jack. "You have been empowered by all who came before you – Bob, the VPs and the management team - to create the first draft of Corporate Insights' Mission Statement." There was a lot of excitement in the room. At the end of the day they stood before a Mission statement that they all signed and proudly handed off for the next employee group to work with.

THE TREE

Toward the end of the day, Jack had them all draw a picture of a tree. When they were done he had them all hold their drawing up for everyone to see. They were all different. Some were pines, others palms, oaks and willows.

Jack explained, "These drawings represent how each of us sees the world. We all see it differently, uniquely. No two trees are alike. And that is our magic as human beings, our uniqueness and creativity. But there are some things we need to understand universally, and how our company works is one of them. It has been my experience that no one in the organization understands exactly how the company works as a whole. Just as we were born into the world and accepted the way things were, so we came into this company and accepted the way things were – accepted without questioning.

"We all have a department-centric view, and even within that, we each have our own individual view. This must change if we are to truly design a game worth playing – a company worth working for. But, change to what? Fortunately, as we found with our beliefs,

---

[11] Code of Honor. As in the Marine Corps. A set of simple, powerful rules that govern the internal behavior of a team, along with the ability of the team itself to enforce these rules. Example: Leave no man behind.

awareness of our current situation is the first step to getting what we want."

By the end of the third day they had articulated organizational work flow and created an *emotional measurement system* that measured mission-critical inputs to their individual departments from their vendors and to their customers.

"This would normally have been a very painful exercise," said one participant, "but somehow all the charge is gone. I know now that all we are doing is reporting on how things were in the past. I know that each of us here today genuinely wants to do better, and the only way we can do that is with a tool like this." The entire group acknowledged the feeling.

Key to the conversation was a simple box that depicted each department. Jack called it "The Boxing Exercise."

To the left of the box were input lines that listed what the department considered mission critical inputs, along with an emotional rating number between one and ten, where ten was considered excellent input. Each input was tied to another department, vendor or customer. It wasn't long before there were a few realizations.

> Working hard had nothing to do with being effective – they were all working hard.
> If our mission critical inputs are not a 10, we have to make up the shortfall up along with our regular workload, causing more hours worked.
> Few departments ever told the input department there was anything wrong, they just complained to others.
> Few departments could say with certainty what their internal customers really wanted because they never asked. They had always done what they had always done and never questioned it.
> While each department rated their inputs low, they rated their outputs high.

BOXING

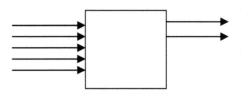

Vendor input (on the left) is a possible 10. Anything less than a 10 leaves the receiving department with a deficit to make up. For example, if an input is a 5, the receiving department must do their 10 plus the missing 5

It was agreed that a full organizational flowchart would be displayed on the company intranet monthly. Each department would rate each of their mission critical inputs each month and post the results on the intranet for the entire organization to see. Surprisingly, the group loved it.

And so it went with Los Angeles, Dallas, New York and London. When they were done, the last group's version would become the Values (see appendix D) and Code of Honor (see appendix E) adopted by the entire company. The degree of empowerment climbed exponentially as the organization realized that London, with a group of 42 contract workers from Bombay, had the final say on the Values and Code of Honor the company would adopt. The tension was so thick you could cut it with a knife. But when London completed their three-day and shared their work product, an amazing transformation occurred when every person in the company adopted their result with only praise.

Shortly after the last retreat, five employees were chosen at random, one from each of the previous five Mission teams. They were charged with integrating the four completed mission statements. Again, when they were finished (see appendix C) and shared their work product, there was nothing but praise for the group. Every employee sentiment was covered. Not a word was changed.

In the end, there wasn't a person in the company who had not contributed to its creation. But more important to Bob, there wasn't a person in the company who wasn't completely aligned with and engaged in his Vision of the future.

CONSIDER

- Creating critical mass – bringing everyone into alignment with the Vision and each other – ensures a new beginning. Jack calls it a Hard Reset. Anything less and you are left with pockets of misunderstanding and festering limiting beliefs.

- Each person in the organization has a Purpose & Passion. Bringing it out and giving it direction makes the unlimited energy of Passion available to the organization.

- Organizations are a mirror of the people in them.

- Organizations hold their own unique set of limiting beliefs.

- These beliefs are invisible until called into question.

- These limiting beliefs adversely affect organizational performance.

- The first step to removing limiting beliefs is the awareness that they exist.

- Relationships are the based upon four simple ingredients and can be managed and grown: common ground; knowing what's expected; knowing where you stand in the relationship; and having the courage and willingness to engage.

- Exploring a relationship may require stepping into your personal power to summon the courage to ask your partner how it's going.

- Do you know how to access your personal power?

- Playing a sustainable game worth playing requires understanding the rules. What are the rules of the game you are playing?

- Creating an exciting game requires the players participate in making up the plays that will be run during the game.

- A Code of Honor maintains integrity and ethics in an organization.

- Employee creation of the Mission ensures buy in and passion for the game.

- "Boxing" opens up conversation between departments at an emotional level and is based on the belief that no one goes to work to do a bad job – employee pride drives cooperation.

CHAPTER 21

THE FIRST 90 DAYS

Transformation happens in an instant.
It's getting the Ego to let go of what it thinks it knows that takes all the time.

The energy began to build after the managers completed their retreat in Atlanta and continued to rise as new groups caught fire, reaching critical mass by the time the program was concluded in London.

Over these five weeks, Bob received over one hundred phone calls and e-mails about the power of the program. He shook his head, thought, "I can't believe we were able to shift this many people so fast. It's like they were thirsty for it to happen…craving it all along. And all we did was give them the opportunity to shine. Remarkable."

The company seemed to explode with ideas, with everyone wanting to upgrade, fix or redesign how they played the Game. At the same time, Bob also acknowledged there were a few bumps in the road, with some of the managers still trying to sort out their new responsibilities. The day-to-day operations and, for that matter, even the re-designed process improvement programs, were being taken on by employee teams eager to make a difference and live into their individual Purposes and Passions. This alarmed some of the managers and even a few of the VP's. They felt out of control, and after two weeks appealed to Bob to slow things down.

"Can't do that, guys," Bob said. "Jack warned us in advance that he would help us turn this company into a 900 pound Gorilla that wanted to dance, and if we were to start the process we damn well better be willing to lead. We are faced with a simple task here: lead, follow or get out of the way."

A few middle managers, especially the career fire fighters, found it hard to let go of doing everything themselves. These were the first to leave the company, and their departure signaled the shift from reaction toward creation within the company.

At the employee team level, there were a few conflicts at first, but the Code of Honor seemed to handle them. Those disputes that did arise seemed to do so because a few people were afraid to use the Code. But over time, once encouraged to access their personal power, even the most cautious individuals began to step forward to voice their perspectives. In one meeting where a participant was having an Ego-challenging episode, one of her colleagues looked at her, smiled, and said, while pulling her arm back, "Why don't you go out for a pass?" After a few brief seconds, he offending party smiled, put her hands up like she was catching the ball and said, "Thank you!" The Code of Honor was used in a spirit of fun and with a great deal of respect.

Soon, Bob noticed that his senior team seemed to relax into their "sponsor" roles, and some of the most significant improvements showed up as better communication among the senior staff itself.

"It just feels better to go to work." said Nancy Cummings, with a genuine excitement. "When ever I go into someone's space, there on the desk is his or her Purpose & Passion statement. It reminds me to speak to that person's Purpose, not their Ego."

Throughout the company, everyone began to relate to one another through the lens of their Purpose and Passion, and two things occurred. First, people became more accountable to their Purpose and Passion, and second, conversations became easier and less stressful because, knowing who they were, people were able to stay centered. There was no need to attack others and no reason to feel attacked – although in truth, old habits die hard.

After 30 days, the results of 'The Boxing' exercise showed up on the company intranet. Using the four-step relationship model, each department took the time to rate how they felt about those providing mission critical inputs to their department. The logic was that if people didn't feel good about their relationship with the other department, something probably wasn't working. The initial result wasn't pretty in some cases. Broadcasting "The Box" results on the company intranet immediately opened up a constructive conversation between the parties because the common ground they equally shared was to *Be Powerful.*

Information became more timely and complete. Instead of chasing down red herrings, teams made progress completing tasks that didn't have to be done over.

Other improvements showed up as a can-do attitude that overcame whatever seemed to be in the way. Individual departments got together and began investigating the more visible processes in the company and when they were finished, over a third of the original processes were dropped or streamlined.

THE 90-DAY REVIEW: PREPARATION

Two weeks prior to the first 90-day review, Bob asked Jack to meet with CI's senior staff to make sure everyone understood the logistics of the process. Everyone was present except Mike Clark, who was traveling with customers, so Bob asked if Doug would take notes and brief Mike on his return. Doug said he would be talking to him later so he's handle the update.

Jack began by unfurling the upside down pyramid on the flip chart that represented the transformative organization. It had the *Be Powerful* Vision statement on it already.

"As you can see, we are operating from a different context than in the past. We have flipped from a directive to a transformative environment." Jack took a moment to scan the group. "How many of you wish you could go back to the old directive way?"

A few of the hands went up and some laughter permeated the meeting.

"Let's begin our time together by Clearing," said Jack. "Nancy, do you mind beginning?

"No, not at all, Jack. Well, I have to admit, while the energy around here is sky high, it has been a little unnerving having my people get together with other departments and hash out issues without me. In two situations all I got was an e-mail from the team leader informing me and my counterpart about a problem and how the team decided to solve it. Now, granted, they said they welcomed my input after the fact. And I didn't have any problem with their decision, it was actually really good. But, I didn't feel I was in control of the group either. I guess I need some coaching on how to be transformative while still knowing what's going on with my own people. It just doesn't feel right." She paused for a moment, and then said "I guess I'm complete."

"Thank you, Nancy," said Jack. "Dave, you're next."

"Yes," said Dave Finney, looking down and very thoughtful. "I think the new way of doing things is, well, new. I find myself walking around looking for a crisis to manage. It's so quiet it feels like I'm missing something, like I'm not earning my keep. I used to be putting out fires and that gave me a sense of importance I guess, but now, well, I seem to have time I never had before. I'm almost wondering if I still have a job."

There was some uneasy laughter.

"So," he continued, "I suggest we get together, just like Nancy said and get some coaching on what else we should or could be doing to make a difference, because most of my complaints have dissipated and I find myself staying late just because I feel uneasy leaving early. My people are working things out with your departments. And if you look at the customer complaint log, the number of unresolved items is down by over half since the retreat."

"Thank you, Dave. Neil, you're next."

"I, for one, am spending a lot more time on M&A activity and loving it. My people have always done a good job for me but now there is nothing for me to do but look outward. They are anticipating what comes next and our managers have been a lot more responsive to their budgets. I guess you can't beat that. If I have any concern, it's about some of the chatter I've been listening to at this level about things moving too fast. When you begin to feel things are out of control, come and see me. Let's talk about it before you try to put the brakes on and disempower yourself. Our people are on a roll and they don't need to be slowed down because we're afraid." Neil looked around the room and paused. "I'm done."

"Excellent. Chris, you're up."

The group was learning to let each other share their feelings without any comment. It was understood that these were just their feelings, so no one needed to say anything, they just needed to share and listen.

"I'm fine," said Chris, "although I have some concern for how much time this 90-day review is going to take. I mean, involving every person in the company is a really big commitment when there is still so much to do. I can see doing something like this yearly, but quarterly, well, I don't think the ROI is worth the time. If it were up to me, I would probably not spend the time."

"Okay," said Jack. He nodded to Bill Peters.

"My guys haven't been quite as spontaneous as the rest of the company. I hope it's not me, but I don't think so. We are making progress but I suspect we still need to stir things up a bit. I'm thinking of bringing Jerry Friars and John Corey back to the team. I think I made a big mistake in letting them go and I've had some preliminary conversations with each of them. They tell me they are open to possibly coming back on the team."

Bill's disclosure caused quite a bit of conversation among the group, but there was little disagreement about his direction. He was encouraged.

"I'd like each of your input on that off line. Other than that I want to thank everyone for their support, I feel like part of this team and it feels good."

"Very good, Bill. Doug, you're next."

"I've been having a ball. And I too want to thank each of you for supporting me in my new role as VP of HR&D. Especially you Nancy, I really appreciate your coaching and support on the EV Project."

"You're welcome, Doug. It's really great working with you as well," said Nancy.

"The EV Project?" asked Chris.

"Yes, EV stands for Enterprise Visibility," replied Doug.

"Nancy took on the executive sponsorship of a new project to encourage use of our own project management software. I never realized all of the limiting beliefs around the issue – what we learned with our own people will help us design a new customer interface model. It's patterned after what we learned in the retreat. Really interesting stuff. I'll fill you all in after this meeting."

"Not another project," said Chris, rolling his eyes.

"I'm complete," said Doug.

Jack nodded to Bob, "Okay, I guess that leaves you, Bob."

Bob took a moment and looked at each of his direct reports. He stood up and walked over to fill his cup with some fresh coffee.

"I remember how resistant I was to Jack when he told me that it would not be difficult to transform myself and the company. I really had to swallow hard to listen to him some of the time. But he also told me that the hardest part would be continuing my own personal transformation, keeping the momentum going and overcoming my own limiting beliefs and self doubt. How did you put it, Jack, the real test of leadership lies with the question 'When you find out what you are here to do, will you have the courage to embrace it?'"

Jack nodded agreement.

"Well, Jack was right; the bulk of my transformation and the company's have happened almost overnight. It certainly surprised the hell out of me. And this uneasiness some of you have referred to in your Clearing – I've had the same feelings. The only difference is, Jack predicted that I would have them and helped me be prepared for that day by 'future pacing' the way I would handle my issues with control."

"Control?" asked Chris

"Yes. There was a time when I wasn't the most trusting soul in the room. But I've learned to let go and trust you guys and you are not letting me down. I suspect if you do the same for your people you will experience similar results."

And what exactly are you doing to let go?" asked Chris.

"Good question, Chris. I guess the most effective thing is reading my Purpose and Passion Statements every morning. When I read them I'm reminded that my job is to generate confidence and self esteem, and you know what, I take that very seriously. It's hard to second guess yourself or others when you remember who you are.

"How many of you remember our Leadership Charter?" asked Bob.

The group nodded that they did, especially since they had updated it to include mission, goals and objectives after the retreats. "Good, let me read the main point of our charter."

> ...to fully engage each other and our people in the powerful execution of our stated Vision...Mission, Goals and Objectives....until at least 90% engagement is reached.

"So I guess one leadership metric is whether or not our people feel truly engaged." said Nancy.

"Good noticing," said Bob. Jack just smiled.

And another metric seems to be our feeling engaged as well, in our own Purpose and Passion," suggested Chris.

"Exactly," said Bob. "As we go forward there is much we still have to learn about creating a transformative, sustainable environment. None of us has done this before. There will be a gigantic learning curve for us as well as our people. But as you are already experiencing, we learn fast." After a thoughtful pause, Bob turned the meeting back to Jack. "I'm complete, Jack. You want to bring us home?"

"Sure thing," said Jack. "You are all exactly where you should be. How you feel is understandable, and there is nothing wrong with where you are. When you have those feelings, just thank your Ego for sharing, and, like Bob said earlier, read your Purpose and Passion statements. Read your Leadership Charter. And as Neil suggested earlier, talk to one another about your issues. And then get back on the program."

"Jack, excuse me," said Chris, "but I seem to be a little confused about the program you're speaking about. I know what we just went through, and while it was interesting and apparently very powerful, I still don't understand where we are going with all this."

"Fair enough," replied Jack, "How many of you feel the same confusion?"

"I won't claim to be a mind reader," said Nancy, "and I don't know exactly what Chris is talking about, but I would like to have a little more concrete plan laid out for us to follow than what we've been doing."

"Very good. How many of you feel the path is a little fuzzy?" asked Jack.

Between the hands, murmurs, and nodding heads Jack had his answer.

"Let me put it into a larger context for you," he began. "During the past 90 days we have embarked on the first of a three phase process of Awareness, Mastery and Legacy. These three levels of success are being applied to three critical success factors: Self, Relationships and the Game.

Level 3: Legacy of self, relationships, and the game
Level 2: Mastery of self, relationships, and the game
Level 1: Awareness of self, relationships, and the game

"The retreats gave us the initial awareness of self, others and the game we are playing. From here on out, each 90 day cycle will test our growth in each area. We are coming up on our first 90 day cycle. You will either feel challenged, appreciated, responsible and part of something meaningful, or you will be asked to change your situation until you do.

"Are you clear about your self, your relationships and the game? Are you in alignment with the rest of the team? Are you engaged?

"What I have just described to you is called *creating the context of the business*. The results we experience are the *content*. Does that make sense to you?" asked Jack.

"I understand the theory," said Chris, "but why didn't you give us this overview up front? And how is the leadership team supposed to behave after this 90-day event?"

"Good questions, Chris," said Jack. "Let me answer each question separately. The reason I didn't share this earlier is that each level of this program gives you a new perspective. Telling you this earlier would not have been productive because you may not have been able to see how it would work without first experiencing the program. Think about it. How many of you really believed that in three days we could re-align and engage people so powerfully?"

The group acknowledged that, while they had done these soft-stuff kind of events in the past, nothing they had ever done was either this fast or seemingly this powerful.

"With regard to your second question, Chris, I can't predict how the leadership team – how you in this room – will behave afterward. In a moment, we'll be talking about what to expect for the 90-day event. What I do know is that organizational performance will be better than ever before. And I know that you have been given a choice between reaction and creation – between your Ego and your Purpose. After looking at some of the progress you and your people are making across a wide front, I would say that most are choosing creation. And my experience has been that once you move the group this far there is no turning back."

"I guess," said Doug, breaking in to the conversation, "it's not what happens, but what we choose to do about what happens that matters. From what I can see, I agree with Jack, we are choosing creation over reaction more often than not, and I for one am comfortable with that."

"Powerfully put Doug," said Jack. "It's not what happens, but what we choose to do about it that matters. So here is the secret to authentic leadership: *respond to what happens through the filter of possibility, not fear.*"

- Come from your Purpose and Passion, not your Ego
- Use the Code of Honor with one another

"Can I get you guys to agree to try that?"
The group agreed that they would try.
"Fair enough," said Jack, "now let's focus on the mechanics of

our first 90-day event, shall we?"

"All of you here and your managers will have been trained in the 90-day CEOing Process before the event," began Jack. "Rebecca has volunteered to coordinate the process and assemble the results for the company-wide meeting to be held on the 18th. It all begins with four key questions that will be asked of individual groups within the company. From your unique perspective:

1. What went well during the past 90 days that we can celebrate?
2. What hasn't gone so well that we can learn from?
3. What are we doing with what we learned?
4. Where are we with our active ON the company improvement projects?

"These questions are designed to engage our people and demonstrate challenge, appreciation, responsibility and being part of something meaningful. It's important that each level in the organization consider these questions as distinct groups. Here is the schedule:

1. Employees assemble in their departments
2. Directors and Managers get together as a group
3. VP's get together as a group
4. CEO gets together with Jack
5. Rebecca compiles the results and reviews with Bob
6. Bob shares results on 90 day CEOing conference call
7. Bob shares the results with the Board

"Why are the groups being split up?" asked Doug.

"Good question. The idea is to capture reality at every level in the company because each level will have a unique perspective. If we are to move toward organizational transparency this is an important step. Especially since we will be empowering each level to address and solve its own problems," said Bob. "In fact, the only time they will need you in the future will be to clear a road block or lobby for a resource."

After a few questions regarding timing, they cleared and the meeting adjourned.

"Jack, can we spend a few minutes clearing before you leave? asked Bob.

"Sure thing."

"I guess I'm surprised at the uneasiness of my senior staff, especially since they also admit that things are getting done at a much faster pace than in the past. I mean we are experiencing amazing results. What do you think is going on?"

"Nothing unusual. You have six VPs and a few have concerns. A few are excited about how things are going and, oh yes, you still have one cynic. Par for the course.

"So what do I do?"

"See, you have some of the same concerns as they do. Like I said, par for the course. The 90-day review and celebration will open up a number of new opportunities and offer a broader and deeper understanding of the process. What say we just let that unfold and then get together for another strategy session? In the meantime, review your original from-and-to strategies and see if you are impacting any of them so far."

"Sounds good. I'll do that. Thanks."

THE FIRST 90-DAY CEOING REVIEW

"I received the completed 90 day report this morning," said Bob to his senior staff, "and I'm amazed at the progress we seem to be making on all fronts. It's all good, and I really appreciate the new Communications Protocol Team's recommendations. One of the original problems identified in the retreats was how the random use of our communications channels was costing the average person 2-3 hours a day, every single day. That's a big number."

"What's the new protocol?" asked Nancy? (see Appendix G)

"It will be released this afternoon, but basically it addresses why, when and how we use specific communications channels.

"For a long time, e-mail was used to pass the buck and cover your butt rather than how the team suggests it be used. In fact the team has given a great deal of thought to how we might more effectively hold meetings and use the telephone, our project management database, and even the online meeting manager."

"Excuse me, Bob, but we're ready," said Rebecca. Team members from around the globe were on the teleconference for the Town Hall and most were also connected on-line through their laptops for the presentations. "And I know you won't believe it, but everyone is accounted for and on-line except those on vacation and two people on maternity leave."

"Excellent, Rebecca, thank you. Is everyone ready?"

His team acknowledged they were and so Bob hit the button to begin. The entire system crashed.

"So much for technology," laughed Bob.

Within ten minutes, however, everyone was back on line.

Bob began. "Depending on where you are, good morning, good afternoon, good evening and good night. For the first time in our history almost the entire company from all over the world is on-line together. This is our first 90-day CEOing review and celebration. This entire broadcast will be recorded and put on our intranet for anyone that misses it. As many of you know already there is a method to our madness. *No more death marches.*"

The line went wild with cheering. Bob was actually a little surprised at the power of the acknowledgement.

Bob continued, "Rather than death marches we will focus all of our energy on creating the kind of organization in which each of us feels challenged, appreciated, responsible and part of something meaningful. Today's review is designed to help us begin. Over the past week each of us has been in meetings that posed four questions."

With that everyone's screens suddenly came alive with a Power Point slide titled:

Being Powerful
1. What went well during the past 90-days we can celebrate?
2. What hasn't gone so well that we can learn from?
3. What are we doing with what we learned?

4.   Where are we with our active ON the company projects?

"I see from the schedule that Development will begin the program," said Bob, "so let's begin." For the next 90 minutes the ball passed from department spokespeople to project team leaders to individuals in the most animated, exciting and fun time anyone could remember in a work environment. Every corner of the company reported results. There were 136 items that went well. These were reported fully on the intranet site, along with public acknowledgement to those involved. The range of successes reported went from adding new customers, to Bill Perry in Engineering and Fred Wilson in Marketing getting together and creating a new product design process. Bill and Fred's accomplishment was especially notable because in the past they had next to no relationship. As a result of the various transformative processes, they had committed to and acted upon being supportive of each other, which resulted in significant progress for each of their departments.

There were also twenty-one things that hadn't gone so well and 6 new projects were proposed to address the root causes of each of these problem areas.

After the last 'didn't go so well' was reported, Doug Martin, VP of Human Development, facilitated an exercise they had all seen in the retreats that tied the 'negative' results they experienced back to an originating belief using the BEAR model. "To change the result, we will have to challenge and change the belief," he concluded.

Bob was thrilled that the $250,000 spent the year before on the Quality initiative was now paying off handsomely, as the quality and continuous improvement tools dovetailed perfectly with the Boxing initiative. Lastly, there were progress reports on the five major structural projects uncovered at the *Be Powerful* retreats three months prior.

1.   The   Communications   Project: Organizing   a communications   protocol   so   that   every   employee   uses communication technology in the most appropriate manner. Potential first year savings in employee time and a reduction in confusion: *$2.16 million annually*

2. The Documentation Project: Adding two new writers and organizing how departments document information and hand it off to the Doc Department. Potential first year savings in people looking for current information, avoiding the confusion and fires not having it causes, supporting customers during release cycles and expanding our ability to support product in Europe where ISO is required: *$1.2 million annually*

3. Product Flow Project: Flow charting each department's operations and creating a "success criteria" for vendor departments in order to improve critical input quality and timing. The objective is to compress cycle times and lengthen development coding time to encourage fewer mistakes. Potential savings in rework and missed opportunity cost annually: *$3.1 to 5 million*

4. Implement CEOing. Building 90-day top-to-bottom reviews into the DNA of the organization. Process designed to keep employees engaged. The 90-day review will continually put employee-generated mission critical initiatives on the table that encourage true 'Enterprise Transparency'. This initiative recognizes the many good employee ideas that previously were buried. Potential productivity gains annually by fully engaging people at every level in working 'on' the company: *$2 to 3 million*

5. Implementing CI's customer software at every level within the company. Uncovering all the ways CI products can be used to improve performance across our enterprise. Improvements in using our own product will improve the end product. 4 and 5 are integrated initiatives. Initiative #4 creates the human willingness to engage fully, while #5 creates the tools and metrics to do so.

Bob knew this was a giant step toward Transparency.

★

CONSIDER

- When you flip from a Directive Organization to a Transformative Organization, employees will take their new responsibilities seriously. If leaders balk the first time employees take responsibility, you can expect some employees to revert back to their old cynical selves. And you can expect still others to remain firm in their determination to make a difference. As a leader, it's up to you to support the latter.

- Calling someone on "their stuff" using the Code of Honor takes courage. You can mitigate the discomfort if, in advance, you ask your team mates what you can say supportively to them that will bring them back to Purpose. They will give you a word or phrase you can use. Use it.

- It's always best to speak to a person's Purpose rather than to their Ego.

- The results of the "Boxing Exercise" posted monthly on the company intranet will do more to fix throughput and quality issues faster than just about any other method. Again, people want to do a good job.

- Every organization has a few mission critical projects that can make all the difference in performance. These are the things that people most need to do their jobs. What are your mission critical issues? Remember, you only have to ask your people.

- The CEOing process of 90-day reviews helps eliminate the negative effects of human entropy and collective ego (homeostasis) and keeps the organization clear, aligned and engaged.

EPILOG

ONE YEAR LATER

Finding out who you really are is the easy part.
Mastering yourself requires on-going practice.

B ob was officially named CEO of Corporate Insights after less than six months in the post.

Once the Board experienced the new *Be Powerful* program they, like everyone associated with the company, became very supportive of Bob's Vision. Bob became the empowered chief executive Jack had talked about.

Two weeks after the first 90 day celebration, Chris asked for a meeting with Bob. They decided to meet at the end of the day in Bob's office. Chris knocked on the door.

"Hi Chris, come on in," said Bob as he moved from around his desk and pulled out a chair for Chris at the round conference table.

Chris took a seat. Bob went to the refrigerator and pulled two bottled waters, handing one to Chris.

"Thanks Bob, appreciate it," said Chris.

"So what's this about?" asked Bob with a look of concern.

"I guess you can consider this meeting my exit interview," he said looking down. "This last year and a half has been very stressful for me, Bob, and since you are into all this Clearing stuff, I thought it would be a good time to let you know how I feel about things."

Bob nodded, waiting for what was next.

"When Jim resigned, I thought I had a good shot at being the new CEO. I don't know if you knew it or not, but I was encouraged by a few of the Board members after he left. As you might expect, I was a little surprised when you got the job, especially since you were in Europe. And after your first meeting with the Board, which, like you told all of us, didn't go so well, I had some further conversations with some of the Board about my candidacy. But then just a week later my support disappeared. You made a hell of a recovery is what they told me."

Bob decided nodding to show he was listening was all he should do for now.

"Since then, well, I've tried to get engaged in your program but find myself observing more than engaging. I get the logic of it intellectually, but I just can't get myself to buy into it emotionally. I'm just not sure if I believe in all the meetings and shifting roles. And the new direction we are taking with our technology, all this transparency stuff, well, I don't believe we need to do all that employee and customer training. The technology is what people buy and that's what I want to focus on. I really don't understand the focus on all the relationship training and how that ties to ROI. I want to build the next application, yet I am being distanced from the critical decisions. Guys I could rely on in the past to do what I told them to do are questioning my directions. Every meeting turns into a discussion. I am becoming less and less effective with this new empowered approach and I can't live with that."

There was continued silence between the two men.

"To be clear, Bob, I appreciate what Jack brought to the company, I really do. While I don't relate to it, I can't deny that he has helped us rapidly change the culture of the company. I just don't happen to agree with the culture we changed to. It's just that I'm a leader, not a facilitator. So, bottom line, I've been developing a project in the entertainment industry. It's not new to me. We've informally talked about my ideas from time to time, but I think the time has finally come for me to act on those ideas. I've finished the network design and economic model and I think we have a compelling story. I'm looking for funding. I will be leaving as soon as you can find my replacement."

Bob waited a moment, and then asked with a smile, "Are you complete, Chris?"

"Yes, I am. I appreciate you listening without interrupting."

"You're welcome, Chris. And thanks for your truthful and candid sharing. Listen, I know that what we are doing has been difficult for you, and yet you have tried to be constructive every step of the way. In fact your questions have helped me dissipate a lot of the natural skepticism for the program. For that, I sincerely thank you. And, I understand your desire to lead in your own way. I hope you find a way to lead from your Purpose and Passion as you look into what's next for you, because you're a hell of a guy. Like Jack has said over and over, his approach is not the only way. But I've come to believe one of Jack's teachings, 'that who you are is what you bring to each situation in life.' Thank you for bringing your authentic self to this meeting. It's made a difference to me."

Chris looked at Bob with a question, like part of him wanted to acknowledge what Bob had just said, but he wasn't sure what that was. He let it go.

"I'd like to get out of here by the end of next month. Is that doable?"

"Do you have a replacement in mind?" asked Bob.

"Actually, I do, especially if you want someone who seems to support and promote the new program. It will probably come as a surprise to you."

Bob looked at Chris with his best inquisitive look, tilted head and all.

"Dave Finney. He's a generalist, and is a hell of a project manager. He's been working with my guys. He's respectful and engaging. He really champions the customer without hitting us over the head with it. Actually gets us to think his approach is our idea. He's earned a new-found respect from the engineering staff, Bob. He might do real well in the new role. And picking someone from inside can't hurt morale any."

Bob was surprised.

"Wow, quite a change of heart Chris. I know you didn't have much regard for him early on. What changed your mind?"

"I just told you. Within the new structure, he fits. He's a collaborator, a facilitator, and no one knows the application or customer requirements better. Well, maybe Nancy," he said.

Bob was really moved by Chris's shift regarding Dave and Nancy. He was compelled to say, "Chris, are you sure you want to leave?"

For the first time in the exchange, Chris smiled.

"It's time." he said, "It's not that I don't appreciate what you're doing here, Bob, I do. But I have this idea burning in my gut that just has to happen. I've been studying the regulatory environment, the available technology, the economic model and the competition and I think we have a distinct advantage by moving now. So, I'm going to go for it."

"Well, if you need more time to make the transition smooth for the family, I'm sure we can work with you on your departure." said Bob.

"Thanks Bob, that's very kind of you. I really hope we can keep in touch."

"I'm sure I haven't heard the last from you, Chris."

The two men shook hands and maintained eye contact. Bob resisted the urge to give Chris a hug, knowing that each of them had a new level of respect and admiration for each other.

The two men parted, knowing it would not be the last time they would see each other.

Over the next few days, Bob shared the news with the rest of his senior staff, especially the part about Dave Finney. Surprisingly, they all agreed that Dave had really blossomed as a leader. They felt he would work into the new role but would probably need coaching. To make sure Dave had the best shot at success, Bob gave a new project to Doug; create an executive development program to help not just Dave, but all managers to grow into their new roles.

Bill Peters, the VP of Sales, took to the new "way of being" and in a highly anticipated move, quickly hired back Jerry Friars and John Corey, two of the sales people he had fired just the year before. They were among the first to complete the *New Employee Course*. Miraculously, two large IT accounts and four major departments within Homeland Security were opened by the duo within 60 days of their arrival. New life was pumped into the pipeline. These successes spurred others on the sales team to victories of their own.

Under her direction, Nancy's Training Group, in cooperation

with Doug Martin, newly promoted to VP of Human Development, created the first *Enterprise Visibility Training Model*. Doug's involvement came out of "Project Number Four" initiated during the retreats to make all CI personnel proficient in CI's signature software usage.

All of CI's personnel were introduced to the EV training model on the occasion of CI's second 90 day review. The initial presentation raised more questions than it answered, but the questions were useful as Doug, working with one of Nancy's trainers, began to bring people through an alpha program and to assimilate the limiting beliefs that showed up with the participants. There were many. But the more CI people who went through the program, the better the new customer version became, and the more engaged they became in their own products.

Customers appreciated the new energy level they were experiencing from CI and were excited about the *Introduction to Enterprise Visibility* (EV) course CI offered users and new customers. It both opened eyes and greatly enhanced system integration and acceptance by users. It was crude by comparison to what they would do in the next year, when they would introduce their new *Introduction to Enterprise Transparency* (ET) course, but it was a powerful step in supporting customers not yet recognized by the competition.

Nancy was promoted to Executive Vice President, giving Bob the time to work exclusively on building the company's future.

Eight department managers, directors and supervisors, including Nancy's and Doug's replacements, were promoted or reassigned within the organization. Two managers were asked to leave because of their unwillingness to let go of blame and complaint. Neither was surprised and both were provided with outplacement coaching to help them through the transition.

The company was writing its own book in its own unique way.

Doug's new Human Development Group focused on three mandates from Bob: *Growth, Mastery and Inclusion*

1. **Growth:** Keep the *Be Powerful* process vibrant by supporting

employee team leaders in identifying and then completing mission critical projects in time for the 90-day review and celebration using CI's software solution.

2. **Mastery:** Provide training, new thinking and practice on CEOing to the leadership and management teams. Personal, relationship and organizational mastery was tied to executive compensation.

3. **Inclusion:** Ensure every new employee completes the *New Employee Course* within 60 days of hire and is fully trained in the company's software and systems.

Over the year, 26 new employees joined the company and they all attended *The New Employee Course*. It introduced them to CI's culture, the three secrets of leadership and the technology that supported the company and its customers.

Several Board members, all of whom completed the *Be Powerful* program themselves, sitting on other Boards, brought this new awareness to other companies.

CI partnered with Jack's company to create an enhanced version of their *Enterprise Transparency* program when three of CI's largest customers requested the new technology.

THE ONE YEAR CELEBRATION

An expanded Board meeting had been scheduled for the day after the one year celebration meeting in Chicago. Bob opened the meeting.

"I would like to begin the meeting by thanking Jack Griffin and his team for the unwavering support they gave us over the past twelve months. We've shared some harrowing moments together but even those were extraordinary in teaching us new ways to lead our company. Jack, you've made a lot of friends here, and we consider you part of the team."

The group applauded Jack loudly.

"And to show our appreciation, and knowing how you love a

flip chart, I want you to accept this memento that declares you and your team an Extraordinary Organization to learn from." Bob handed Jack a rolled up flip chart sheet with the declaration signed by every employee in the company. The group again applauded Jack and his team. "This flip chart page must have at least 50,000 miles on it."

"I love it. Thanks Bob, and thank you all for your courage and determination to create something so powerful. It's been a real pleasure working with you," returned Jack, "and I want to acknowledge how much we have learned from you as well."

"Does that mean we get a discount?" kidded Nancy.

The group laughed.

When the group quieted down, Bob continued, "I want to share some metrics with you. We are ending the year 16% up in sales and 36% up in profit over last year. And while sales and profit are up, the manpower needed to achieve it is down dramatically. The death marches are truly over and overtime is down by over 40%. The average employee worked 56 hours a week a year ago and is working 46.5 today.

"Our stock price has stabilized at $36/share, not bad considering we were at $23 just seven months ago. The new Enterprise Visibility Program has gotten excellent press and 80% of our customers are signed up to participate in the latest system updates. Many of you have participated in Nancy's and Doug's 2.0 version of the EV program that we will be re-naming ET for *Enterprise Transparency*. We will be offering the three-day Enterprise Transparency Workshop to our customer base along with the 5.6 release in March."

"And as you can tell from yesterday's proceedings, we have no tolerance for complaint in the company; if something is not working, or if people are dissatisfied with anything, they are fully equipped and empowered to fix it. During the past 12 months Neil has monitored every project taken on by staff. He captured the time necessary to address each project and subtracted that cost from the projected ROI. The amount put to the bottom line by the top 5 projects coming out of the initial retreats paid for the cost of the Be

Powerful Program six times."

The group applauded and congratulated each other.

"During the first three quarters we had over 75 projects put forth and completed. And while we have several new projects in the hopper for this quarter, it's nothing like it was just a few months ago. Heck, it won't be long before you will have more time on your hands, and I wouldn't doubt that some of you will begin wondering if you'll have a job next year."

The group laughed, with Dave Finney commenting "Just when I started to go home at a decent hour and feel secure about it!"

Bob laughed at that.

"Listen, I think we all agree we're operating powerfully. I am really proud of every person in the company. I've never had so much fun seeing people as engaged as they are. We've learned a lot about ourselves, our relationships with one another, and the game we call Corporate Insights. And I think we are ready to go to yet another level, what do you think?"

The Leadership Team looked around the room at one another and noticed the Board members sitting back with smiles on their faces. Something was up.

"Neil and I have been working with the Board on another acquisition. The company is called *PhaseMatics*. They're actually bigger than we are in revenue and head count, but they've been running hard and have been demoralized for a long time. There's a lot to do to assimilate, rebuild and revitalize them, but I think we can do this. "

"Oh good grief," said Nancy rolling her eyes in jest, "here we go again!"

"That's right Nancy," said Bob, with a faint grin and a glint of excitement in his eyes. "Here we go again."

THE END

CONSIDER

A. The Three Secrets of Leadership work together to form a solid foundation of growth, mastery and inclusion.

B. The New Employee Course will keep the organization from sliding back in to an Ego Driven organization by constantly bringing newly liberated people to the mix.

C. Organizational growth goes through predictable stages. Do you know where you are?

D. According to the NY Board of Trade, over 90% of all Acquisitions and Mergers fail to meet their intended goals. The primary reason for failure is an inability to realign and engage the new entity fast enough.

E. A Transformed organization understands how to bring a demoralized directive organization back to health. After all, they've done it themselves.

APPENDIX

A. Corporate Insights Vision

B. VP Leadership Charter

C. Corporate Insights Mission

D. Corporate Insights Values

E. Corporate Insights Code of Honor

F. Corporate Transformation Map (The seven steps to Creating an Extraordinary Organization)

G. The Communication Project Protocol (A breakthrough in getting the most out of technology in communicating within an organization)

A. The Corporate Insights Vision

Be Powerful
Powerful People, Process, Results

B. The Corporate Insights Leadership Charter

We are the Corporate Insights Leadership team.

Our Charter is to fully engage each other and our people in the powerful execution of our stated Vision, Mission, Goals and Objectives.

We will know we are truly engaging our people when employees report, through an independent employee survey, at least a 10% quarterly improvement in the degree to which employees feel challenged, appreciated, responsible and part of something meaningful, until at least 90% engagement is reached.

Signed,
The Corporate Insights Leadership Team

C. Corporate Insights Mission

We are Corporate Insights, project software development and implementation experts. Our Purpose is to empower and transform large organizations by creating software solutions and innovative implementation strategies that make enterprise visibility and, ultimately, enterprise transparency, a reliable reality for clients. Our solutions enable them to identify the profitable combination of the right ideas, the right efforts, and the right measures, that maximize the value of their people, projects and portfolios.

Short version:
We are Corporate Insights. We maximize the value of people, projects and portfolios.
Signed,
The Employees of Corporate Insights, Inc.

D. Corporate Insights Values

These Values were created by the employees of CI in order to guide our actions in living into our Vision and Mission. The intent of these Values is to build powerful people and relationships and to ensure we always uphold a powerful customer orientation, both internally and externally. Being Powerful – We honor and live our personal and corporate Vision with confidence, passion and effectiveness focused on relationships, innovation and achievement.

- Integrity – We keep our word. If we find we cannot keep our word we let someone know in time to do something about it. If we fail to keep our word, we take full responsibility for it and do not blame anyone else. We learn to say no.
- Professional Fulfillment – We expect to be challenged, appreciated, responsible and part of something meaningful.
- Respect – We value diverse talents, perspectives and ideas with openness and curiosity.
- Understanding – We strive to recognize content within its proper context by listening to understand and speaking to be understood.
- Thoughtfulness – We approach each decision and task with due care, respect, consideration and reflection.
- Openness – We promote self expression with confidence, being receptive and responsive to ideas, and free communication both within and across organizations.
- Leadership – We strive to empower, inspire and engage others with a passionate Vision of success.

We believe honoring these values will empower and unite all CI members to learn, grow and achieve in serving a Purpose worthy of our effort.

Signed,
The Employees of Corporate Insights

E. Corporate Insights Code of Honor

The CI Code of Honor was developed by CI Employees to represent how we will conduct ourselves professionally and provide a basis for effective engagement.

- Be confident and have faith in one another.
- Be engaged in the process as part of the solution, fulfilling our commitments, and supporting group agreements.
- Be specific when making requests, providing status and feedback, and managing expectations by giving complete, relevant and accurate information.
- Be accountable for our actions and take responsibility for our word. Recognize and ask for help when needed. Say no when appropriate.
- Be process oriented. Be aware of, use and continuously improve our existing processes and change them with our peers when they no longer serve our mission.
- Be innovative in our execution and deliverables, knowing that our ideas will be encouraged and nurtured.
- Be a leader, coach and mentor by sharing experiences and lessons learned, setting positive examples and inspiring others by providing opportunities and removing barriers.
- Be respectful of others and their ideas, identity, culture and time by listening, learning, and growing from their input and diversity.
- Be considerate of others in meetings and communications. Be on time. Be responsive to requests no matter how they come to us. Be attentive and provide open, unbiased listening. Be sensitive to time zones.

Signed,
The Employees of Corporate Insights, Inc.

F. CORPORATE TRANSFORMATION MAP

Phase 1: Hard Reset

1. CEO Transformation* and creation of the Corporate Vision and Strategic Plan
2. VP Transformation and Alignment with the Vision and Strategic Plan and the creation of a Leadership Charter
3. Manager Transformation and Alignment with the Vision, Strategic Plan and Leadership Charter and the initial draft of Corporate Values and Code of Honor
4. Employee Transformation and Alignment behind the Vision, Leadership Charter. Further refinement of Values and Code of Honor. Creation of the Corporate Mission

Phase 2: Sustainability

5. Specific Projects that continually re-design corporate structures to be in support of the culture's full engagement in the Strategic Plan
6. On-going 90 Day CEOing Ritual to reinforce being challenged, appreciated, responsible and part of something meaningful
7. The New Employee Course welcomes new employees into the organization by helping them articulate their own Purpose & Passion statement while introducing them to the unique story of CI's Vision, Mission, Values, Code of Honor and Strategic Plan

*Note: *In this context, transformation means that each participant has experienced the Three Secrets of Leadership: They have articulated and are working on mastering self; they foster a compassionate understanding of humanity and are engaged in mastering relationships; they feel passionate about what they are doing and are fully engaged in playing a Game that is meaningful to them.*

G. THE COMMUNICATIONS PROJECT[12]

As Powerful people, we seek to fulfill our personal Purpose and Corporate Vision and Mission by adhering to our stated Values and Code of Honor. Our ability to communicate effectively with others, both internally and externally, is essential to our success. This means having complete, accurate and actionable information at the right time, and avoiding the overload of non-essential or ego generated communications.

Recognizing the challenges presented by our geographically distributed organization (which include time zone differences and minimal face-to-face interaction), we will facilitate better communication by properly using the following tools:

INSTANT MESSAGING:

We use Instant Messaging (IM) to get someone's immediate attention to ask simple/ quick questions, point people to information and schedule communications. We do this by first asking permission to interrupt them when we start the communication. We don't use IM to interrupt others when they are otherwise engaged, or to make "ego driven" comments during meetings or conference calls. To facilitate our usage, we will maintain our IM "Status" (e.g. Online, Busy, On a Call, etc.) to help others better communicate with us.

E-MAIL:

We use Email for distribution of information, interchange of questions and answers and explanations, for less-formal communications that should be documented, scheduling communications, and to point people to information on the CI Intranet or other databases. We will be conscious of others time to read through email sending only to relevant parties, using "cc" for those based on true need, using "reply all" with discretion,

---

[12] These are actual results from a live project

following proper escalation channels as required, and not using email as the "CYA" informal escalation. We include phone numbers and pertinent contact information in our emails, and use Out-of-Office messaging if we are to be on a known absence.

CI INTRANET:

At the center of our corporate collaboration and knowledge is our CI Intranet, which we use to house information common to all CI employees and/or cross-functional groups. The CI Intranet is not expected be used in place of specialized databases. (Sales Force CRM for example) Recognizing that all Corporate Insights employees have access to the CI Intranet, it is preferred that we not distribute attachments (Word, PowerPoint, Excel, Visio) via email- but post documents to the CI Intranet and send a Notification email to others indicating availability. We will appropriately label documents as DRAFT and update the Version History as we revise so others can determine its state of completion. We use the CI Intranet to document actions, deliverables, and status; to share, collaborate and document decisions.

TELEPHONE:

We use the Telephone for communications that do not require "visuals" or extensive supporting detail, and for matters of timely importance. If we are placed into voice mail, we will let the person know how we can be reached that day (if required). We all agree to respond to our voice mail messages on a daily basis. We use voice messages and telephone contact for situations requiring timely attention to a matter given that some team members may not be able to respond to e-mail communications promptly. To respect others' time and responsibilities, we will schedule conference calls in advance. We will be conscientious and, if we are to be away, will make sure that an extended absence greeting is used.

FACE-TO FACE

We will use Face-To-Face communication when reasonable and primarily for kicking off a new project, brainstorming, problem solving, and crisis management—especially when the team members are in the same office. Face-to-face should not be used in place of responsibly documenting information and consideration must be given to help maximize productivity of all team members-being careful to not interrupt or distract. Sometimes a phone call is sufficient; use judgment.

WEBEX/CONFERENCE CALLS:

Webex and/or Conference Calls help mitigate our geographic diversity and work well for some situations requiring in-depth problem analysis, discussion, planning, brainstorming, design, decision-making and training. Invitations to participate in Webex or conference calls shall include Webex meeting names, passwords and conference call phone numbers. PowerPoint is a good tool to help communicate via Webex and should be used to clarify points and/or capture ideas. Presentations should not be unnecessarily complex or lengthy, and the visual technology should enhance the communication of the message, not distract from it. When appropriate, we "share control" of documents and presentations to facilitate idea exchange and mutual understanding.

INDEX

ABOUT THE AUTHOR

TOM VOCCOLA is Co-Founder and CEO of CEO^2, a Chief Executive consulting firm specializing in Executive Team Alignment and Accelerated Cultural Transformation. Over the past fifteen years, Tom and his team have utilized the very secrets revealed in this book to assist hundreds of CEOs and executives throughout the United Stares, Japan and Europe, in transforming their lives, their organizations, and the lives of the people they lead.

An entrepreneur, and an Accidental CEO of three companies himself, Tom is an accomplished speaker, and co-founder and past Chairman of the Los Angeles area CEO Roundtable for the American Electronics Association. An avid sailor, Tom sails his Classic 44 Mercer sloop *Sea Fever* out of Ventura harbor. He lives with his wife, best friend and CEO^2 co-creator, Frances Fujii, in Thousand Oaks, California. You can reach Tom and his company at **www.ceo2.com**.

Made in the USA